The Dynamic Manager's Guide
To Practical Management:

How To Manage Money, People,
And Yourself
To Increase Your Company's Profits

By Dave Donelson

THE DYNAMIC MANAGER'S GUIDE
TO PRACTICAL MANAGEMENT:
How To Manage Money, People, And Yourself
To Increase Your Company's Profits

FIRST EDITION

ISBN-10: 1463782055
ISBN-13: 978-1463782054

This book is also available as an eBook ISBN: 978-1466135536

Acknowledgements
Some of the material in this book originally appeared in various forms
in one or more of these publications:

914Inc
Accessory & Performance Retailer
Automotive Aftermarket
Autographics
Broadcasting & Cable
Central NY Business Journal
The Christian Science Monitor
Club Industry
Convenience Store Decisions
Distribution Sales & Management
Distribution Channels
Electronic Media
Entrepreneur
Fabricator
Family Business

Gift Basket Review
LP Gas Magazine
NFIB's MyBusiness
Niche Magazine
NSGA Retail Focus
Nursery Retailer
Performance Business
Pizza Today
Professional Builder
Restyling
Ward's Dealer Business
Westchester Magazine
Woodworker's Journal
Woodshop News

Table of Contents

About This Book

Successfully managing a business large or small takes knowledge, skill, and a fair amount of guts. Luck doesn't hurt, either. Management is an occupation not for the faint of heart, nor for those whose goal every day is to spend eight hours collecting a paycheck while expending as little effort as possible. Really, really good managers do whatever is needed to keep their business operating at top form—and then some.

I've been involved in management as an entrepreneur, consultant, and journalist, not to mention the years I spent running companies for other people before I set out on my own, yet I continue to be amazed at the range of skills a manager needs to succeed. He or she has to understand finances, bookkeeping, budgeting, and working capital formation. They need to know how to hire, train, and motivate the best employees—and fire the other kind. A good manager has to grasp the basics of marketing, advertising, merchandising, and customer service. He or she also must deal with investors, partners, vendors, the press, landlords, tax collectors, and sometimes even family members. Good managers have to be a specialist in their industry and a generalist in their professional skills. Management success demands life-long learning.

I hope The Dynamic Manager's Guide To Practical Management will be part of that continual learning process for you. Like all the books in the Dynamic Manager series, it is short on theory and long on practice. Not that there's anything wrong with studying the "why" of management, but few managers I know have much time for academic pursuits. They need answers—now.

Sometimes they even need questions! When a business is floundering or stagnating, even the best managers don't always know where to look for a problem they can solve or a new path they can follow. They often need someone with whom they can brainstorm, compare methods, or even just swap war stories. In its own way, this book can help.

It is based on conversations and interviews with hundreds of managers and business owners across the country. They include retailers, manufacturers, service providers, wholesalers, restaurateurs, and many others. They market everything from picture frames to race cars, janitorial supplies to sporting goods to insurance. They have union and non-union workforces (and sometimes none at all!). They operate in single-car garages and multi-story office buildings, mega malls, and downtown storefronts. Their stories of success—and failure—contain lessons for managers in every industry.

Like all the books in the Dynamic Manager series, this one is designed to be sipped, not swallowed in one big gulp. It's full of thought-starters. Read a chapter or two and think about it a bit before you go on to the next one. See if you can identify ways the situations faced by the managers in the book match the ones you encounter every day in your business. Try their solutions—or your variations on them—to see if they apply. I hope you'll keep coming back for more.

--Dave Donelson

Section One

Financing Your Company

Running a successful business is all about the money—where to find it, how to manage it, how to make and keep more of it. Sound company finances don't just happen, you have to plan for them. In this section, we explore financial planning, show you how to find cash for your business, and explain how to manage your money through good times and bad.

Inadequate funding causes most business failures. Good financial management will not only keep your company afloat, but enable it to grow and prosper.

Chapter 1
Don't Just Hope For Success, Plan For It
"If you expect to run a profitable business,
you need a business plan."

A business plan is your map to the money. It tells you where you're going to get it and how much of it you're going to be able to keep. And just like any map, the more detail the plan has, the easier it makes it to get to your destination.

Do you need a business plan? Would you hire someone to remodel your kitchen who didn't have a set of blueprints? I'm sure you wouldn't think of it. So why run a business without a plan? Unfortunately, it happens all the time, which may be the reason well over 500,000 businesses fail every year.

Most of the small business owners I deal with really know their craft. They know what materials to use, which vendors offer the best terms, which customer is most likely to complain, and so on. They're also pretty good business people. They understand controlling expenses, tracking labor and material, and pricing their product to make a profit. They work hard and are justifiably proud of the results.

Their business plans, though, all too often sound like "If I build it, they will come." That may work in the movies, but it stands as much chance for success as a plan to install a tonneau cover that doesn't include the model number of the truck.

Why plan?

If you expect to run a profitable business, you need a business plan for many of the same reasons you need a plan to remodel a house. It helps you focus on the important factors that contribute to success. It helps you make key decisions on everything from the types of work you look for to the number of employees (if any) that you hire. A sound business plan is also an absolute must if you are looking for capital, whether it be from investors, banks, or even suppliers.

A concrete business plan identifies the customers, quantifies the sales they will produce, and analyzes how profitable those sales will be. It's like a job estimate that begins at the end of the process (the sale to the customer) and works backward. It helps you determine how much material to order and how much labor to plan on, project the costs, and figure out whether the job will be profitable at the price quoted. Only, instead of doing it on a job-by-job basis like an estimate, the business plan does it for your company as a whole over a period of time.

Plan components

A business plan isn't really about what kind of work you're going to do or how much shop space you need. Those are elements of it, but they are so minor that they're almost footnotes. There are five basic components:

1. Business Description – A short statement about why the business exists and what it hopes to accomplish. Generally, the more specific—and shorter—the better.

2. Marketing Plan – Answers the questions about how the business will be successful. Who is going to buy the product or service? Why? What need does it satisfy? How many potential customers for it are there? How often will they buy? What are their competitive alternatives? What price will they pay? How will they know about it? How will you get it to them?

3. Financial Plan – Shows the expected financial results of the marketing plan. How much income will be produced? What net worth will be generated? Who will receive that income (you or the bank)?

4. Cash Flow Plan – The step-by-step instructions for generating cash and keeping it. How will the working assets be acquired? When will operating cash be needed? How soon will profits appear? What happens until then?

5. Management Plan – Describes the shop owner or manager's role in the business. Who will do what? What are their qualifications? How much training expense and time is required? How much time will be devoted to production, marketing, and administration? It also includes contingency plans for events like natural disasters, up- and downturns in the economy, and competitive changes.

This very brief description of each component is not at all complete but it should give you a flavor of what kind of information, hard data, guesstimates, and reasoning go into the business plan. Most of all, a good business plan needs to be grounded in reality, not wishes. I like to say that it should produce an optimistic outlook based on pessimistic expectations.

Preparing a good plan doesn't happen over a lunch hour. It requires research and thought. Sound business plans can come in many forms, but they all have one thing in common: they are in writing. Whether you use one of the many good software packages available or fill up a loose-leaf binder with pencil-written notes, the act of writing it down forces you to give your plan the time and thought it deserves.

Who needs it?

Many people think of a business plan as something that only a start-up needs. But that's like saying that once I look under the hood and start overhauling my engine, I won't find any little hidden surprises under the manifold or behind the old water pump. If my garage does body work, I may have replaced acres of body panels, but I know there are going to be surprises just as sure as a paint gun makes overspray. When a surprise occurs, I can turn to my plan, make the necessary adjustments, and—most importantly— trace the ripple effect those adjustments will have on the rest of the business. Having a blueprint—a business plan—saves me time and eliminates a bunch of errors.

A well thought-out business plan is also essential if your company is to grow. Growth requires capital for things like more space, more machinery, more people, more material, more everything— that will hopefully lead to more profit. That capital may be available from the company's current revenue or the owner's bank account, but most of the time it's going to have to come from a loan, vendor credit, or even outside investors. Any one of these sources are going to require not just a financial history of the business, but financial projections as well. Projections supported by the business plan.

But what if there aren't any outsiders to deal with? Even if the money is coming out of the owner's pocket, the decision to reach in there and get it should be based on a sound plan as well. Most good business people I know are justifiably stricter about spending their own money than they are about spending anybody else's. That's how they got that money in their pocket in the first place.

Plan help

One final analogy: Preparing a sound business plan is a lot like installing bath tubs—it's usually a heck of a lot easier if there are two of you there to do it. Fortunately, there is a wealth of help available. The Small Business Administration is a starting point for information and connections to other resources. Look for a local SCORE chapter (Service Core of Retired Executives) or a SBDC (Small Business Development Council) through your Chamber of Commerce, community college, or public library. Your banker or accountant may be able to provide some direction, too.

Chapter 2
Where To Find Money
"You can get the capital you need
if you invest a little time in thinking."

"It takes money to make money" may be the truest axiom since "measure twice, cut once." But look at that first statement closely. Nowhere does it say whose money it takes. If you need capital for your business (and who doesn't?), for new equipment, materials, or to even-out the spikes in your cash flow, there are several places to get it other than your own wallet.

Let's start, though, with the single worst source of funds: your credit cards. Unless you are sure you can pay the balance off in full before the end of the month (and if you could do that, you proba-bly wouldn't need to be borrowing the money in the first place), the interest is going to kill you. You won't last long if you borrow money at 18% (or more!) to build a product where the net after-tax profit margin is 10%. And, no, you won't make it up on volume.

Many entrepreneurs look to family and friends for loans, es-pecially when they are starting up their company because it's tough (although not impossible) to borrow money from a bank or credit union to start a business. Ignoring the personal relationships in-volved, personal loans are viable options not to be overlooked. They often carry lower interest rates and generally have a less formal approval process than those from standard financial institutions. There are a few IRS rules to watch out for, though, and there are about a thousand reasons to have a legally-binding written loan agreement signed, so consult with your attorney or tax advisor before Aunt Sadie reaches into her cookie jar.

Going to the bank

For larger or longer loans—or if you want to avoid the psychological quagmire of borrowing money from your brother-in-law—you'll want to turn to the people whose purpose in life is lending money: banks, credit unions, and savings & loans. The thought of going through the loan application and approval process can be very off-putting, but it's kind of like spinach; you may not like it but you're a better person for eating it. The process of compiling the necessary information and thinking through your proposal will help you focus on some important shop management factors.

It may not seem like it, but banks are actually eager to loan you money because that's where they make their profits. These institutions will grant your loan if you can show that your business proposal is sound. They will turn your loan down, however, if they judge you to be a bad credit risk. While your personal credit history may be a factor in the decision, most of the time bank loans are denied because the proposal was inadequate or poorly presented. Your shop's financial history alone is generally not sufficient proof that the loan you're requesting is secure. For that, you need to show that the future of the business is rosy enough to make the probability of repayment very high.

Don't even think about applying for a loan unless you know exactly how much money you need, what you need it for, and how you will pay it back. Every one of those items will need to be substantiated in some way, too. How much money you need is directly related to the amount of cash your shop generates now, so you'll obviously need up-to-date financial statements (backed up by a CPA's analysis and/or tax returns). What you need it for comes from your marketing plan and answers questions like who is going to buy the product you are going to make and the likelihood of their purchase based on competition, pricing, the economy, past purchases, etc. The question of how you will pay it back is answered by your cash flow projections.

Collateral

Assuming your proposal answers all the pertinent questions, your financial institution is probably still going to ask for some sort of collateral and/or a personal guarantee. The collateral, of course, may include the assets (equipment and inventory) of your business, real estate, marketable securities, or other tangibles the financial institution can sell if they have to. They probably won't consider as collateral the value of your company as a going concern—because they don't want to operate it, which is what the bank would have to do if they took over your business in the event of a failure.

The personal guarantee is slightly different. A lien against your home, bank account, or other personal assets assures the bank not so much that they can recoup their money in the event of a failure, but that you have a strong incentive to keep running your shop and living up to the terms of the loan. They know it's much easier for the borrower to walk away and leave the bank holding his unsold inventory than it is to give up his car.

What's sometimes thought of as another source of capital really isn't. The Small Business Administration doesn't make loans—it guarantees them. You first apply to your bank or other financial institution for a loan the way I've just described. The bank may choose to make the loan on its own, or decide the loan requires additional support in the form of an SBA guaranty. They will then request SBA backing. The SBA does not secure 100% of the loan amount, either. The financial institution is still going to have to come up with at least 15-25% of the funds. The SBA also requires collateral, personal guarantees, and a sound credit history.

Short-term solution

Another option for raising working capital is a form of asset-based lending called "factoring." This can be an expensive source of funds but it's not without its uses, especially in case of short-term emergencies. A factor essentially buys your accounts receivable at a discount today, and you turn over the entire balance to them when it is collected tomorrow. The difference, of course, is the factor's profit and your cost of capital. One thing to keep in mind is that, since the factoring company is assuming the risk that your customer won't pay, they are seldom patient with past-due accounts. Since these may be customers with whom you want a long-term relationship, any heavy-handed collection techniques can backfire on you.

It's entirely understandable, considering the uncertain state of the economy, that many of us are reluctant to take on new or additional debt. If you have a sound business plan that takes the current economic conditions into account, though, now may actually be a good time to borrow to grow your shop's business. Your competitors may be laying low, so it's easier to gain market share. Your prospective customers are very receptive to value propositions. What's more, now is an excellent time to get capital to fund your growth. Financial institutions are becoming more eager to make loans (no loans, no profits) and interest rates are at historic lows.

You can get the capital you need if you invest a little of your time in thinking through the situation before going to the bank. Anticipate the questions that will need to be answered, explore all the options, and put together a professional-looking, thoroughly-documented proposal. Then you'll be able to make money the best way—with someone else's money.

Chapter 3
Is Cash King?
"It's your attitude toward debt that counts"

In today's economy, a small business is wise to hang on to cash. But despite its obvious advantages, the 'cash is king' strategy won't necessarily result in a strong, sustainable company. What really matters is a company's attitude toward debt.

They may feel like they are slipping back to an era when men wore fedoras and women's dresses seldom rose above the calf, but more and more small business owners are recalling their fathers' mantra that "cash is king." As family business consultant James E. Barrett points out, "Suddenly, the old man who was considered stodgy and overly conservative is looking pretty damn smart."

Those tales from the past always seemed to carry the lesson that cash should rule because it's quantifiably certain—either it's there or it's not. There is a lot to be said for verifiable assets in a business climate where supposedly rock-solid resources (and even landmark financial institutions) disappear overnight.

"Relationships are great, but cash flow is even better," Jacob Wallenberg, a fifth-generation member of the family that controls Swedish bank Skandinaviska Enskilda Banken (SEB) and giant holding company Investor AB, recently told The Economist (Jan. 24-30, 2009). The publication noted that both SEB and Investor

AB are holding their own in the current economic crisis. Investor's more than 80 holdings include interests in industrial banking systems manufacturer ABB, drug firm AstraZeneca, and manufacturing and construction equipment firm Atlas Copco. "The main reason for Investor's resilience," The Economist reported, "is that it entered the downturn flush with cash, giving it the means to support struggling subsidiaries and buy distressed assets at knockdown prices."

But, like most aphorisms, "cash is king" can't be followed slavishly in all situations. "If you are talking short-term, it's absolutely true," says Barrett of Cresheim, Inc. in Philadelphia. "If you're talking the longer term, thinking is king—cash helps."

Another point to keep in mind, according to many advisers, is that while running a business on a strictly cash basis may seem like the safest way to operate, it's not necessarily going to result in a company that's stronger or more enduring than one that makes judicious use of debt. And it may not even be possible! Even the most conservative managers would be hard-pressed to operate without at least some use of other people's money, be it vendor terms for merchandise, a mortgage that unlocks the value of the company's real estate, or a bank credit line to help with seasonal variations in the operating cash flow.

All debt is not created equal

"We use the term 'debt' as if all debts were equal," says Fort Worth, Texas-based family business consultant Sam Lane of the Aspen Family Business Group. "That's simply not true. There is debt used to cover losses, but it's not the same as debt that simply levels out bubbles in demand or debt that's used to finance equipment. Those are very different kinds of things."

And what about growth? Few businesses generate enough free cash to fully finance the acquisition of a competitor, build a new plant or upgrade a manufacturing facility without using some sort of long-term debt. They may not go to the bank or Wall Street, but seller financing, borrowing against an insurance policy and factoring receivables are forms of leverage also.

During the buyout boom, the Wallenbergs' Investor AB, the largest industrial holding company in the Nordic region, was criticized for being slow to make deals and for sitting on too much cash, The Economist noted. But the company's family-controlled status enabled Investor to stick to its strategy. Investor "could resist pressure from outside investors, because it is almost impossible to take over," the article said.

Yet despite family firms' advantages in a climate where Wall Street investors are incessantly calling for quarterly profits, family business leaders face some challenges that CEOs of non-family companies don't have to worry about. David Thompson, CEO of Laminators Inc., in Hatfield, Pa., points to one of the most common in explaining a major shift on his balance sheet that occurred last year: "We had a very substantial cushion, but it was built up for a cash-out event for my father. Two of my brothers and I used the equity to take out a loan to buy the business." It was the first significant debt the company had incurred in more than 40 years.

Watch your leverage; curb your lifestyle

Barrett summarizes the most widely held view of the regal status of cash when he says, "The better approach is not so much having cash as not getting too highly leveraged."

Jack Mitchell knows about that firsthand. He says his family's company narrowly averted disaster in the 1989-91 recession and took steps to make sure it never happened again. The second-generation owner and CEO of Mitchells/Richards, a high-end fashion retailer in Connecticut, tells a grim tale: "We had debt as the recession started. We had to do warehouse sales to raise cash. It was totally contrary to our brand, but we needed the cash." He says the family found themselves in that position because they had just finished expanding their original store in Westport, CT, and acquired some property next door for another expansion when the recession started. "Thankfully, our advisory board said we absolutely shouldn't take on any more debt and, in fact, we should be cutting back on what we had and building our cash reserves," Mitchell recalls. "For a while, I didn't like that answer, but I'm sure glad we followed it."

Today, Mitchell proclaims, "We believe in three Cs: customers, community, and cash."

It's worth noting that the company has some real estate debt and works with its vendors for the most favorable terms possible, but it generally depends on its own cash flow to finance operations. While Mitchell won't discuss the details of the company's 2005 acquisition of Marsh's, a retailer on Long Island, he says no significant debt was added to the balance sheet by the transaction.

Mitchell also points out that his company avoids one can of worms commonly opened by other family businesses: excess cash distributions. Even though seven family members (including Jack's brother Bill and his wife, Linda, as well as four next-generation members) work in the company, "We try to preserve the cash we have as a backup," Jack Mitchell says. That practice has proved very sound in recent months, since many of the stores' customers are Wall Streeters, who these days are as careful with their purchases as Main Street denizens are. "They don't wake up every morning feeling compelled to go buy a cashmere sweater," Mitchell laments.

In many multigenerational business families, "There is a strong dynamic that money left in the business is money that the owner can't put in his pocket," notes family business consultant Sam Lane. "That's why you'll find many family businesses with run-down equipment and things like that."

But Sean Smith, who in 1995 founded Coalition America, an Atlanta health care resource management company, with his twin brother, Scott, says too many family business owners are using their businesses as personal piggybanks. "I see a lot of family businesses that are really lifestyle businesses for the owners," Smith says. "They'll put cars, houses, retreats and a lot of personal things on their company that don't really add value to the company. What it does is give them ways to improve their lifestyles."

Though the Smith twins were just 26 years old when they founded Coalition America, which helps clients manage health care costs, "We've always run this as a business," Sean Smith says. "We don't even have cars on the company."

In that respect, a non-family business may hold an edge over a family firm, notes Lane. "In a non-family business, management can't do that [extract money from the company]. They get their salary and their bonus and that's it. They can't take money out otherwise." Those who attempt to do so end up with a damaged reputation, as former Merrill Lynch CEO John Thain learned when reports of his $1.2 million office renovation became public.

Smith says he and his brother learned the value of cash at their mother's knee. "It's rare that my mom will buy anything unless it's on sale," he says. "I can remember having a savings account from the time I was three or four. I remember going to the bank to deposit 35 cents over the counter and watch my passbook balance go from $1.60 to $1.95."

While they don't use the company's funds to finance their lifestyle, the Smith brothers haven't found it necessary to retain excess cash flow in the business, Sean Smith says. Instead, they've chosen to pay bonuses and make distributions over the years. "My brother and I and some of the employees who are also shareholders own 100% of the business," Smith says, "and we've been able to pull out enough capital over the last 14 years to diversify our portfolios." Their personal finances are sound because of the company, but not dependent on it, Smith says. "If the company were to disappear tomorrow, I would be stressed," he says, "but I could still maintain the lifestyle I want."

Smith uses a gambling analogy to explain his philosophy. "We could leave cash in the company to compound, but it's kind of like going to Vegas," he says. "If you're ahead, do you let it all ride, or do you take some of the winnings off the table? If you sit at the table long enough, you'll probably wish you'd put a few of those chips in your pocket."

It should be noted, however, that the Smiths' company isn't capital-intensive. They must meet payroll for about 100 employees and keep up their investment in IT, but unlike many firms, they don't have heavy equipment, inventories or other cash traps.

Smith and his brother may have strong feelings about cash, but they didn't hesitate in 2008 to take a major plunge into the debt markets to finance their $25 million acquisition of National Preferred Provider Network, a major strategic move that Sean Smith says has paid off already. "That has ended up being a very good acquisition," he reflects. "It increased our client base and gave us a large base of contracted providers to give to our clients. It gave us a lift in revenue and EBITDA as well as adding to our service platform."

They chose to make the acquisition with a five-year note from GE Capital so they wouldn't have to dilute their equity by issuing additional stock, Sean Smith says. "We've been able to pay that down in the first year by almost a third," he adds. "We're well ahead of schedule."

Fiscal discipline

The Smith brothers' experience may be the exception that proves the rule, according to Lane. "You've got to have a real race horse to operate at the edges of leverage," the consultant says. "You need to be in an industry or run a company with an extremely high growth rate to outrun the debt service. Most family businesses just aren't like that." He adds, "I've seen family businesses that are leveraged to the hilt, and most of them just aren't that high-performing."

Barrett urges caution, too, especially today. "If you look at the companies in difficulty now, most of them could do fine on an operating basis, but they got themselves so highly leveraged that they have big payments coming due and they cannot muster the amount necessary. They also can't roll them over because the banks are being so fussy or they don't have the collateral."

That's the scenario that weighs heavily on Thompson's mind after his buyout of his father. "We're starting to feel the pinch like the rest of the world," he says. "We typically have a $1 million backlog going into a month, but there have been recent months where we've started with only $100,000."

His company, Laminators Inc., serves two markets. It bonds plastics and metal into sheet panels for outdoor signs, like those used by real-estate agents, that are sold around the Western Hemisphere through a distributor network. Laminators also manufactures composite panels used in commercial construction for decorative wall systems—usually around the entrance of a building, often surrounding a glass storefront. Revenue is split equally between the two lines of business. Both have been affected by the current economic downturn.

"We laid off some folks, cut everybody's hours back to 32, and my office staff is taking a 10% pay cut," Thompson explains. "It's not fun, but if you do it right and do it early, you can keep yourself from ending up in a great big hole." In the summer,

Thompson says, the company typically employs about 90 people. Business is slower in the winter, and the firm sheds seasonal help as the weather cools. In recent months, Laminators has had had two layoffs, cutting the staff to about 75.

The company's debt—the first in its 40-year history—could crimp future growth, too, particularly the expansion of some product lines that Thompson has in his sights for when the economy turns around. In the meantime, it will definitely limit the owner's ability to pay dividends. "We have covenants in our loan that include cash flow recapture," Thompson says. "Until our ratios are above a certain trigger point, we as owners are precluded from taking distributions beyond what it takes to pay the taxes. Anything above the trigger, the bank gets 25% that goes toward principal reduction."

The economy is pushing more companies into cash-centric strategies just like Thompson's. "People do everything they can to conserve cash," Barrett points out. "They cut the inventory, reduce people, fiddle with pricing and credit. On the customer side, you can either shut credit down or extend it to keep customers alive. Inbound, business owners work with their own suppliers to improve their terms and work with their banks to maintain their financial ratios within the covenants of their loans."

On a more sophisticated level, Barrett adds, "Losses, and tax refunds on the basis of them, are a source of cash. There is room to play in those areas, and the accountants know about it."

It sometimes takes a little fancy footwork and more than a modicum of discipline, but there are definite advantages for family businesses who put cash back on the throne. "Probably a third of my clients have no debt whatsoever, aside from a small line of credit," Lane observes. "They sleep well at night."

"There's a new reality out there, and we have to adjust to it," says clothier Jack Mitchell. "That's how we'll have a business to pass on to the fourth generation."

Originally published in Family Business www.familybusinessmagazine.com.

Chapter 4
Case Study: Serial Acquisitions
"Pitfalls and profits from growth by acquisition"

Robroy Industries is a family business built through serial acquisition. In fact, every product the 103-year-old industrial conglomerate sells today is produced by one of the 17 companies acquired by the second and third generations of the McIlroy family. As the fourth generation prepares to assume leadership at company headquarters in Verona, PA, near Pittsburgh, they're planning to follow the acquisitive path.

That strategy has served the company well in many ways, according to chairman and CEO Peter McIlroy, grandson and namesake of the founder. Robroy has used it to diversify against risk, expand product lines and increase market share, fueling a steady growth in sales to well over $100 million annually and generating profit margins approaching 20%, truly spectacular for a basically low-tech industrial manufacturer. With no debt on the balance sheet and five strong years behind it, the company is poised for further expansion.

The McIlroy acquisition strategy has been handed off from generation to generation like a baton in a relay race. Peter's father, Bob, brought him into the company in 1965 as a "floor boy" in one of the plants; in 1977, he masterminded his first acquisition under his father's watchful eye. Peter's own sons joined the company in the 1990's and helped in the takeover of two rival companies in 2001 and 2003 under the tutelage of Peter and Company COO David Marshall. They've accepted the baton and are preparing to carry it down the next stretch.

Though acquiring companies has been effective for Robroy, the deal-making has not always been executed perfectly. "Sometimes we got it right and sometimes we didn't," the 65-year-old McIlroy volunteers. "Sometimes we thought a company was in a niche that fit our business and had potential for good margins. After we bought them, we found our assumptions were not correct." Several of the 17 companies bought since 1961 turned out to be less than perfect fits; one or two of them were out-and-out disasters that threatened the company's survival. Even those acquisitions were valuable, though, in that important lessons were learned.

Early growth

It all began when patriarch Peter McIlroy, the current CEO's grandfather, emigrated from Adiewell, Scotland, to McKeesport, PA, where he landed a job in a steel mill earning five cents an hour as a machine operator. In 1905, he and a partner (whose estate sold its interest to the McIlroys after his death in 1950) founded Enameled Metals Company in a garage in Etna, PA. Their product, an innovative paint coating, proved to be a boon to another new product just coming on the market, steel conduit used to carry electrical wires. The company had its ups and downs, surviving the Great Depression, labor problems, fires and even the Great Flood of 1936, where water rose so high it flooded the vats of enamel in the company plant and floated it all over the town of Etna. When the waters receded, everything in town had a coat of shiny black paint.

When Bob McIlroy, one of Peter's three sons, was named president in 1953, a relentless expansion of operations began that has continued to this day. The first acquisition was in 1961, when a manufacturer's rep suggested the McIlroys look at a tiny Texas company that was putting plastic coating on Robroy's steel conduit. Bob bought Houston Coating and Bonding for $25,000. The product it manufactured, Plasti-Bond Coated Conduit, is Robroy's premium line today.

That acquisition also established the pattern for many of the successful deals to come. Not long after the takeover, the Houston plant was closed and the manufacturing operation moved into a new plant that Bob had built earlier in Gilmer, Texas. In 1967, the company became Robroy Industries, freeing it from identification with one product. The name was a combination of Bob's name "Rob" and the "Roy" in McIlroy. Bob's son, Peter, became president in 1980, CEO in 1988 and chairman in 1993.

A three-legged company

Robroy is essentially a stool with three acquired legs. The coated conduit business is the strongest of the three, representing about 65% of sales. It was shored up considerably by the two acquisitions in 2001 and 2003, which gave the company three of the four leading brands in the business and an estimated 50% to 60% share of the market, according to Rob McIlroy, one of Peter's two sons. The only competitor in the coated conduit business is Ocal, a product line offered by $2 billion electrical industry behemoth Thomas & Betts.

The other two legs are roughly equal. Stahlin Non-Metallic Electrical Enclosures was acquired in 1977, and Duoline Technologies was bought in 1985. Stahlin makes molded fiberglass and plastic junction boxes from 3 to 90 inches tall, while Duoline produces corrosion-resistant PVC and fiberglass lining for oilfield steel tubing. Peter's older son, Jeff, 41, has most recently served as the International Business Manager for Stahlin, which he says gave him a great appreciation of how important it is to uphold operational standards of excellence.

The two electrical product divisions serve the industrial construction and civil infrastructure markets. Peter says these markets are countercyclical, so the company hasn't been much affected by the recent slowdown in residential and commercial construction. The oil field business, of course, is very strong, although he reports current problems with hiring a workforce in that labor-starved industry.

Learning from mistakes

While these and several smaller companies turned out to be good buys for Robroy, not every venture produced the desired results. The failures generally followed a pattern. The target companies tended to resemble Robroy's other manufacturing businesses and used some of the same processes so it would appear that synergies--that well-known buzzword of the M&A world—were plentiful. But large problems arose when Robroy tried to compete in markets where it had no experience.

One of the first missteps was Warren Corporation, a company that made metal laboratory furniture. It was acquired in 1963 and moved into the then-unused Verona plant. It was never successful and eventually closed down. In the late '80s, Robroy bought a metal enclosure business thinking it would fit with the fiberglass box operation. "It turned out to be such a commodity business that we eventually sold it," Peter explains.

The worst foray into uncharted waters, though, was the 1990 acquisition of Trimm, a company that made computer enclosures. "That was really outside our core competency," says David Marshall, Robroy's president and COO.

The thinking at the time was that Robroy would be able to add value to the product through engineering, according to Peter. But, he says, "it turned out the customers saw it as a commodity and the pricing was very unattractive. On top of that, we're kind of an old-line meat-and-potatoes business, and we're not swift enough to develop products for the high-tech computer industry."

There were internal problems, too, Peter adds. "We couldn't integrate Trimm, for example, in terms of marketing and manufacturing," he notes. "There were some similarities in metal fabricating, but the culture in the computer industry was totally different. It stood alone because there was no connection with anything else we did. We even had trouble integrating them from an IT standpoint."

Another factor that undermined Trimm's success was the largest intangible of all, according to Robroy CFO Mike Deane. "It all goes back to the people equation," he says. "The people who came along with it weren't creative and talented and diligent."

On the positive side, Peter says, the Trimm fiasco demonstrated the wisdom of diversification of risk: "We had a lot of losses during that period that lowered our net worth. If our other divisions hadn't been so strong, we would have been out of business."

It was ten years before the Robroy team made its next move. When they did, they applied all the lessons learned to make sure the next acquisitions were successful. According to Peter, "The three most important things are, one, buy the right business, one that's profitable as opposed to one that's inherently low margin and trying to change it. Two, install operational excellence. Three, have a corporate culture of your own choosing. If you don't develop a corporate culture, one will be developed for you that you might not like."

Easy integration

PermaCote and KorKap, the coated conduit competitors acquired in 2001 and 2003, were almost the exact opposites of Trimm. "We knew what we were buying," Deane explains. "We were very familiar with the products, the market and the customer base. In addition, we were able to plug them into our current operation, which was fantastic. We were able to take advantage of economies of scale, throughputs and absorption. We were able to add volume without adding any fixed costs."

Essentially, when they bought the two companies, all Robroy acquired were the brand names, customers and distribution relationships. As Rob McIlroy points out, "We bought no bricks-and-mortar, no people, not even any machinery." Without any acquired employees, there was no need to integrate benefit plans, payroll records and the like, much less deal with the attitudes and culture of another workforce.

Robroy didn't even bother to acquire the work-in-progress inventory of the companies, according to Marshall. "If you have, say 2% of the value of your inventory in WIP, the cost of trying to handle that may be more than it's worth," he explains. Since Robroy didn't buy the physical plants, it made no sense to move half-finished products to Gilmore.

The plants and employees may have been jettisoned, but the customers weren't, according to Marshall, who says a major part of the company's planning for an acquisition is ensuring that as many buyers are retained as possible. It's not difficult, he says, if you recognize a key principle: "The customers aren't really attached to a company; they're attached to the goods and services they provide. For most customers, the fear is that change will cause disruption. If you eliminate that, the customer base adapts very quickly. Ensuring that you do nothing to diminish and everything to enhance the service they receive really makes it simple."

Integrating systems

Robroy also worked to maintain the acquired companies' distribution networks, since the company has exclusive representation deals with distributors in the coated conduit lines. "Today," Peter says, "we won't acquire anything unless we're prepared to integrate them quickly and fully into our information systems. Having access to an enormous amount of information on a real-time basis is so important in this company because of our performance measurements leading to operational excellence. We could never get that in a company we acquire if we can't use our own information systems quickly."

"You really have a choice," Marshall explains. "Do you operate more than one IT system, which will add cost somewhere, or do you standardize the system and adapt the people's behavior? It is probably, long-term, a lot easier to adapt the user's behavior."

All Robroy divisions are run using the same off-the-shelf software package and the acquisitions are integrated into it on Day One, a tactic that was adopted with the PermaCote and KorKap takeovers. "There were some challenges with our bills of material, our part numbers, and our order entry," Deane recalls, "but once we overcame those, it was pretty much plugged in."

As little as possible is left to chance, according to Marshall, who says the takeover planning itself takes 60 to 90 days and occurs while the due diligence is going on. "You're learning and planning at the same time," he says. "You're not trying to attack all the issues the day the deal is done. If you identify the priorities and think through the issues around the priorities, you're not taken by surprise."

The company decentralized operational management in 1995, another lesson about absorbing acquisitions learned the hard way. "By decentralizing and putting one person in charge of each business, we got accountability and speeded up the process of making decisions," Peter says. The company went from 58 people at headquarters to 14 today.

Planning for the future

As you might imagine, surprises aren't high on Peter McIlroy's hit parade, so he's working on a long-range succession plan already. Peter will retire when 57-year-old David Marshall retires, he says, but that's not happening anytime soon. In preparation, though, Peter's two sons moved back to headquarters specifically to gain experience in corporate affairs after working in operations since the early 1990s. Jeff, 41, has been with Stahlin, while Rob has been leading national sales for the coated conduit companies.

"They haven't seen what goes on in acquisitions, what goes on in legal battles, accounting, IT, the other things that are centralized here," Peter explains. Robroy has fought its share of legal battles, particularly with unions, including one that landed on the front page of the Wall Street Journal in 1937. Strikes in the late 1950's caused them to close the Verona plant for two years and actually prompted the eventual move of manufacturing operations to Texas. "My goal is to let them see the non-operational side of the business and to work with me so they're prepared to make their own decisions when the time comes."

Peter's son, Jeff, confirms that the future almost certainly holds more acquisitions for Robroy Industries. "We're never satisfied with the status quo," he says. "A lot of family businesses that reach the fourth generation kind of peter out. My brother and I are very committed to seeing this company continue to grow profitably."

Originally published in Family Business, www.familybusinessmagazine.com.

Section Two
Company Strategies

Good managers step back to get a wider view of their company from time to time. They make sure it responds to the market and stays on the path to maximum profits. To make the hard decisions that lead to success, the small business manager needs a variety of skills, knowledge of his or her industry, and a strong grasp of business strategy.

Some of us fight change and some of us embrace it, but we all have to deal with it. This section covers a variety of management techniques to manage change while maximizing profits.

Chapter 5
Change Is In The Air Everywhere
"Some of us fight change and some of us embrace it,
but we all have to deal with it."

Nothing is so permanent as change. The customer you deal with today will not be the same one you see tomorrow. Your employees will have a different outlook on work when they get up in the morning and your vendors will come through the door with new products, new prices, and oh, by the way, new corporate owners with new credit requirements. More of your tools will have LCD screens and many of them will talk wirelessly to your customer and to each other. You can only hope they keep talking to you. In every type of business—change happens.

Some of us fight change and some of us embrace it, but we all have to deal with it. "You have to respond to the market," says Michael Young, owner of Street Rods by Michael in Shelbyville, Tennessee. "If you can't adapt, you're not going to be here in five years."

Consider your customers. Most company owners are justifiably very proud of having a base of loyal customers. If they rely exclusively on those loyal customers to support their revenue stream, though, it won't be long before they see their sales decline. Why? Because customers change. Consider just one simple fact:

twenty percent of Americans move every year. While not every one of them moves across the country and therefore out of your market area, many do. And even those that just move across the street put a dent in their disposable income with moving expenses, etc., that cut into their budget for other things—like what you sell. Those lost sales have to be replaced by sales to new customers just to stay even.

Even the customers who do stick around change. Their tastes evolve, they learn new things, they get bored and want to do or own something different. If nothing else, they get older. The baby boomers, the generation that gave us the Rat Fink and American Graffiti, has started cashing Social Security checks. How will that change their propensity to spend money on hot tubs, designer denims, or flat screen TVs? And will the younger customers who hopefully come along to replace them be looking for the same things? Not likely. That's one reason you see more muscle cars on the street and fewer '34 Fords; more Hondas and fewer Chevrolets. It's not just a change in fashion—it's a change in the customer.

Don't fight it

So how do you deal with change? To start with, don't fight it—you can't win. Instead, open your eyes to the inevitability of change, make yourself and your company ready for it, and embrace it when it comes. The first step, if you want to keep up with changes in the marketplace, is to make a conscious effort to listen to what the customers are saying to you about themselves and what they want.

"Customers are more knowledgeable," observes Sales Manager Tom Dickinson of AP Tuning in Lebanon, PA, a company that specializes in high-performance automotive work. Not too many years ago, hot rod magazines and mail-order catalogs defined media for that market. Today, enthusiasts can learn about the sport from an ever-growing number of media outlets—everything from the Internet to entire television networks devoted to it. Enter a term like "torque converter" into Google, and you'll get 743,000 listings. When Dickinson's customers see somebody on TV winning races or shows with a car like theirs, they become a more informed—and generally more demanding—customer.

"It used to be that you learned about cars by talking to the guy in the next pit stall at the track," according to Darrick Klima, also in the automotive performance business as owner of Belleville Motorsports in Belleville, KS, where they build over 100 race cars a year. "One of the bigger things these days are race car workshops and driving schools. People are spending money to become better racers because they're spending more money on better race cars. It puts a lot of pressure on everybody." Klima attends schools and seminars himself so he will know what his customers are being told.

Klima also spends a lot of time getting feedback from customers. "We meet change by listening to our customers," he says. "All I do all day is talk to people who are racing our cars." He says he and his staff listen to the drivers' ideas, bounce them around internally, then try them out to see if they work. If they do, the new concepts become incorporated into all their products. "We have to definitely spend more time and money trying to come up with a better mousetrap."

Change affects everybody

Don't forget to prepare your staff for change as well. I've never talked to a company owner who didn't say that finding good people is one of the hardest jobs they have. Once you've found them, they'll be a lot more valuable to you if you invest in training them to use the newest technology and encourage them to keep their eyes and ears open to new ideas in your industry. Employees that receive periodic training have a higher sense of self-worth, feel greater loyalty to their employer, and perform at a higher level, so your investment in their training will pay for itself many times over.

The market changes in other ways, such as when new competitors enter the fray. With the growth of the Internet, anybody willing to spend ten dollars a month to host a website can proclaim themselves your competitor and start selling to your market online. As Dickinson points out, "The drop-shippers online put additional pressure on shops like ours. It's tough to tell a customer we have to charge him $500 for a part when they can buy it from some Joe Schmoe online for $400." To respond, AP Tuning added full online shopping capability to their own website. It's not a major factor in the business—yet—but it helps meet the changing marketplace conditions.

Young went online in 1997 and today has a website that not only sells parts, shows off customers' cars, and gives you a wealth of information about the business, but even allows you to "build your car" online, changing various components and getting a rough quote on cost. He has one staff member dedicated full time to keeping the site up to date. "The Internet has paid for itself two hundred times over," he says.

You don't necessarily want to be on the bleeding edge of change, but you do have to fully commit to changing your operation when the time comes. That probably means making a financial commitment to new tools, training for your people, or even new shop facilities. The smart shop owner who recognizes that change is going to happen budgets for it, setting aside something every month in a contingency fund or establishing a line of credit to be tapped to meet changes in the market. You may not be able to specify today what you'll need that money for tomorrow, but you can rest assured that you are going to need it for something.

Change will never stop—it will always happen. LP's became cassettes that were replaced by CD's that lost out to tunes downloaded to iPod's. As of a couple of years ago, Western Union no longer sends telegrams. Monday Night Football moved to cable. Next year, who knows—maybe your customers will become your competitors. Will you be ready?

Chapter 6

Temptation By The Numbers

"This new frangelator system will double your shop's profits. Just sign here."

The salesman's pitch is very seductive: You can make a gazillion dollars just by adding his company's product line to your existing specialty. Maybe your shop has built a reputation for professional work, specialized installations, and custom designs. You've built a good business, but the exponential growth you experienced in the early years has tapered off to single digits. You make a nice profit, but wouldn't it be even nicer to make more?

Sure it would! But is adding another specialty the best way to do it? Maybe, maybe not. The only way to decide is by getting out the old calculator (or opening a spreadsheet on your computer) and doing a little ROI analysis before you sign up for that new fictional frangelator machine and a supply of frangels, whatever they are.

It's one of management's age-old quandaries. Is it better to focus your business on what it does best, growing it organically and building your profit margin by ever-improving efficiencies? Or does it make more sense to diversify, to have a basket full of businesses so that if one falls off another one can take up the slack. You can certainly make strong argument for either approach.

But the basis of any discussion of changing your business mix has to be a careful, thorough analysis of the ROI, or return on investment, of all the alternatives. It's not hard, but there are a few less-than-apparent factors you should consider.

First estimate your profit

The first step is estimating the size of the frangelator market by answering a couple of questions: How many customers in your area could use one and, of those, how many are likely to buy one?

Depending on what you're considering, the first question can be answered with a little research into your market that fit the criteria. Let's say you're in the automotive aftermarket—a place for frangelators if I ever saw one. If the product is model specific, fitting only 1999 model year or later Ford Explorers, for example, you may be able to do something as simple as checking with the department of motor vehicles to find out how many of them are licensed to your market. The key thing to get, though, is a specific number; there isn't any "a lot" key on your calculator.

The second question is a little trickier and may require pushing the frangelator salesman for some information about sales for existing dealers in similar markets. If he's not forthcoming, ask him for some dealer names and numbers so you can check with them yourself. A few phone calls to confirm the company's performance in terms of delivery, support, and reliability would be a good idea anyway. While you're at it, find out how many frangelators they sold in the first year.

Now calculate the potential revenue you can bring in. If there are 1,000 potential customers in your market and you can sell ten percent of them in the first year, multiply the price of the item by 100. Subtract the product costs, labor, and other direct expenses, and you have the potential first year gross profit. Then do the same math for subsequent years, too, assuming some reasonable growth in the number of units sold for up to five years. Average the five-year gross profit and put that number aside for a minute. Some variation on this is probably the basis of the frangelator salesman's pitch, by the way.

Then estimate your investment

But now let's do the other part of the ROI equation. How much will you have to invest to produce this new profit? Here's where it gets a little tricky because there are some hidden costs that are easy to overlook and, quite frankly, sometimes difficult to quantify. The investment in more shop space, equipment, necessary parts inventory, etc., is pretty straightforward, of course. But there are other, less tangible, costs associated with any new venture.

What about training? Will the company send someone to your shop to show you and your people how to install those miraculous frangels? Do they provide training off site? Or at an existing dealer? What's it going to cost you to get that training? Even if the company doesn't charge for it, your people don't work for nothing, so any time they spend learning the ins and outs of the frangelator business is on your payroll. Their wages, benefits, etc., can't be ignored (nor can yours), nor can any out-of-pocket travel expenses related to the training process.

There is another employee-related cost that is easy to overlook. Everybody's time is money and so is yours. Unless you have some pretty special employees, they can't be working to satisfy existing customers' needs while they are becoming frangel experts. Count up every man hour you expect to invest in training and multiply it by the amount of revenue your employees generate per hour, and add it to the direct training cost.

Then there's marketing. You have to let the 1,000 people who own frangelator-needy vehicles know that you can help them. If it's a new product, you may have to spend some money explaining what it does and why they should have one. What's it going to cost to reach that target market the number of times necessary to get the message across? Whether you choose mass media like TV, radio, or billboards, or targeted ones like direct mail or email, there are substantial costs involved in producing the message and buying the media.

It's tempting to say that you don't need to spend any money advertising a new product because your existing customers will line up to buy it themselves and/or tell all their friends about it. That's a hope, not a business strategy. Don't be penny wise and pound foolish in this department, because skimping on the marketing will simply reduce your potential sales. The company may provide some help, of course, so take advantage of all of it you can get.

Add the direct investment in equipment, parts, etc., to the training and marketing costs, and that's the size of your investment. (For the sake of simplicity, we're going to assume that you won't need further capital investment in subsequent years.) Your investment gets pretty large pretty quickly when you add these other factors into the equation, doesn't it? Funny how the frangel salesman didn't mention them. But there's nothing wrong with large investments if the return justifies them.

Finally, calculate your return

To calculate the ROI, simply divide the average annual gross profit by the total investment. You'll get a percentage that tells you whether it makes sense for your shop to go into the frangelator business.

Here are the Frangelator number for the automotive aftermarket shop I've been using as an example:

Size of Market - 1,000 vehicles

Average Annual Unit Sales – 150 (15% of the market)

Gross Profit Per Unit - $50

Average Annual Gross Profit (150 X $50) = $7500

Estimating the investment

Equipment, parts, etc. - $5,000

Training (salaries plus lost revenue) - $12,000

Initial Marketing - $3,000

Total investment - $20,000

Return on Investment ($7,500 / $20,000) = 37.5%

What's the cutoff point between a wise decision and a foolish one? That depends on your tolerance for risk.

If the return is less than what you'd get by investing the same money in a ten-year US Treasury Bond (around 3% as of this writing), don't even think about it. In fact, unless it's substantially greater than what you could earn from other less-hassle (although never risk-free) investments like stocks (assume 10% for the long term), it probably doesn't make much sense, either.

On the other hand, there are other returns on an investment in a new product or service line that are truly impossible to plug into an equation. What's it going to do for employee morale? Will it bring in new customers that will buy something else while they're there? Will offering a cutting-edge, up-to-the minute device like a frangel make your company stand out from the competition? The answers to any of these questions will help you make a wise investment decision.

Chapter 7

Details, Details, Details

"Attention to detail matters to your customers, too."

Ask anybody who spends their day in a furniture finishing spray booth, and they'll tell you ninety percent of success in a paint job comes from attention to detail. Proper sanding, masking, tacking, priming, and so on are mandatory. So is a clean gun, properly mixed paint, and the right temperature in the spray booth. Skip a step or give it a half-baked effort, and you're going to find sags, clouds, over-sprays, fisheyes, and other ugly features in your finish coat. Your attention to detail is what matters.

The same is true when it comes to running your business. Just as a perfectly-applied finish coat depends on what came before it, a successful business depends on dozens of factors other than the ability of the company to produce eye-popping work. Profit doesn't just magically appear. It's the result of constant attention to the large number of details involved in running a successful business. Unfortunately, like sanding between finish coats, most of these details aren't things many people consider fun.

How much do you enjoy bookkeeping, for example? About as much as you like root canal, right? You know it has to be done, but you'd just as soon not do it yourself. I know plenty of company owners who approach the job of keeping their books by throwing all their receipts, invoices, and bank statements into a big box. When tax time rolls around, they dump the box on their accountant's desk and wait for the bad news. This approach is about as effective as throwing an old sheet over a sofa and calling it re-upholstered.

As tedious as it is, keeping a timely set of books will help you run a company with much higher profits. And with the availability of easy-to-learn software, you don't need to be a CPA to master the basics. Even if you're lucky enough to have an office manager who handles the task, it's a good idea to personally review the results every month. Good, timely bookkeeping will help you spot profit leaks before they become floods.

If you review your books in detail, you can plot the costs of materials or labor over time to see if there are any negative trends developing. You probably have a good sense of what's happening, but it's never a bad idea to have the specifics in front of you before you make any decisions. You can also spot cash flow glitches and accounts receivable problems before they occur so you can take the appropriate steps after considering all the alternatives. It's always better to talk to your banker about a loan before you're in crisis mode.

You may also have a nice surprise in store when tax time rolls around. If your accountant doesn't have to wade through your box of dusty documents, he or she should charge you a lot less to prepare your tax return. And who knows? Your diligence throughout the year may actually enable you to lower your tax bill by shifting expenses or revenues—quite legitimately—from one year to the next, by making a timely retirement plan contribution, or by using other time-sensitive strategies of the tax-wise. You can only do those things if you've paid attention to the details of your bookkeeping.

Keeping personnel records is another business detail that's about as much fun as jabbing a letter opener under your thumbnail. If you don't keep accurate personnel records, you're not only asking for trouble but missing an opportunity to keep your staff motivated. Yes, there is a positive side to employment paperwork.

When was the last time you gave good ol' Charlie a raise? How large were the Christmas bonuses last year? How close is the new guy to finishing his probationary period? You may be able to keep all these details in your steel-trap mind, but you're probably better off if you write them down and keep them organized somewhere handy instead. If you typically give annual raises, for example, good ol' Charlie may be expecting his the first of the next month. You may not remember when his anniversary is, but I guarantee you he does. Miss the date, and Charlie may mope around for a month before he tells you what's bothering him. On a more proactive, positive note, if you get everybody together and not only hand out the Christmas bonuses but remind them that this year's is ten percent higher than last, you'll get a bigger bang for your bonus buck.

Of course, maintaining accurate employment records is an essential detail from the government's standpoint, too. Wage and hour records, payroll taxes, and immigration documents may not be at the top of your hit parade, but certain bureaucrats live and breathe them. If they want to see yours, the files better be in good order or it will cost you. Keep in mind, too, that even if you have someone else handle this paperwork, you (or your corporation) are legally responsible for it, so at least check it over periodically to see that everything is shipshape.

Attention to detail matters to your customers, too. If you install sun roofs in cars, the fact that you will vacuum the entire interior after the job is a given, but did someone remember to call the customer to let them know their car is ready? You probably wash a customer's car before allowing the customer to see it, but do you show them the car before you present the bill? Little things go a long, long way toward building a company's reputation for good work—and not all of them are related to your technical skills.

How detailed are your estimates, work orders, and invoices? The more detail you provide on your paperwork, the greater the confidence your customer has in your professionalism and the fewer disputes you will be forced to mediate. Another benefit is that your staff will be less likely to overlook something if it's in writing—or to accidentally do something to the customer's property that wasn't ordered. Mistakes are expensive.

While we're being picayunish about paperwork, have you tried to read your own handwriting lately? Mine seems to get worse with each passing year—and it wasn't too hot to start with. If you provide hand-written estimates that look like they were written in Sanskrit, you're asking for trouble. Try block printing instead of cursive script if you have to. Or, better yet, check out some of the management software packages that will let you print out a neatly typed—readable—document for your customer.

Details, details, details. They're a pain in the behind, but they're also key to running a company where the bottom line is in growth mode.

Chapter 8

Negotiate Your Way To Profits

"Make Better Tactical Buying Decisions"

Mention negotiating to some people, and the first image that comes to mind is a table full of lawyers and accountants haggling over a billion-dollar contract. In most small companies, you seldom get involved in those kinds of deals, but you do conduct negotiations of many kinds all day every day—sometimes without even realizing it. You negotiate with suppliers, customers, service providers, even employees. You give and take over everything from delivery dates and financing terms to whose turn it is to clean the coffee pot in the break room. Perhaps the most important negotiations, though, are the ones you conduct with vendors and suppliers. How well you perform there can make a major impact on your company's success.

Obviously, being a good negotiator can improve your bottom line. Less obviously, though, when you improve your negotiation skills you also reduce some of the stress that comes along with running a business. You'll enjoy both wider profit margins and fewer headaches if you're prepared for the negotiating process and ready to use your skills when the need arises. Before you begin a negotiating session, you need two things: information and a game plan.

Information is something you can't have too much of. You need to know as much about the other person's needs and wants as you do about your own. If you are negotiating with a vendor, how's their business? Is this sale important to them or just routine? Are they operating under competitive pressure in the marketplace or do they have a monopoly? Is their plant running at full capacity? Is their warehouse bulging with unsold inventory? Is the rep over quota or desperate for a sale? Some of these things you can find out by asking them directly or just listening closely to casual conversation; others will take a little research in the trade press or a reading between the lines in your dealing with competitive vendors. In either case, the more you know in advance, the better off you'll be.

Look at your own situation ahead of time, too. Get the facts and figures straight about what you need, when you need it, how much you're willing to pay for it, and so on. The more solid information you have, the more confident you will be in making decisions—and such confidence will greatly influence the way the vendor responds to your offers.

Remember, too, that this information is as confidential as your bank account numbers. You don't need to reveal it to the vendor unless it's going to help you get something you want.

Plan the give and take

Successful negotiation is by definition a matter of give and take, which is where the planning comes in. Preparing a list in advance of the possible concessions you can make as well as a list of things you'd like to have in return is often a good idea. The list will help you prioritize your requests and make sure you don't overlook any possibilities. As you're drawing up your list, remember that negotiation isn't just about price. Delivery schedules, payment terms, packaging and displays, advertising allowances, return policies, and many other elements can add (or subtract) value to the transaction. And nearly every one of them is negotiable, so it never hurts to ask.

You can also offer the vendor some items he or she might want besides a higher price, too. The size of the order comes to mind right away, of course, but what's it worth to them to get a quick decision from you? Or how about payment in advance? While you normally don't want to tie up your capital, if the price of the parts or merchandise you're buying can be slashed below the cost of the money (the interest you would earn if you kept the money in the bank for the time it takes to sell turn the inventory, to look at it simply), it might make sense.

One of the preparatory steps I always found useful was to think through my final position—my least acceptable alternative—before I started negotiating. This might include the highest price I could afford to pay, the largest quantity I could justify ordering, the longest delivery date I could accept, and so on. I would try to include every factor that might come up and decide—in advance—the worst terms I could accept before walking away from the deal.

What we're talking about here is my "take it or leave it" offer. I would certainly never reveal it to the vendor, but knowing where I stood gave me a scale on which to measure possible concessions that I was either willing to make or that the vendor offered as the negotiation continued. Knowing the ultimate bottom line ahead of time also kept me from making costly mistakes in the heat of the moment.

The other thing to prepare in advance is a wish list of everything you could possibly want from the vendor. Don't keep anything off the list just because you think "they'll never go for that." You don't know unless you ask!

Make your concessions count

When the actual negotiations begin, this preparation will pay off if you follow a few simple guidelines. First, ask for the vendor's price, terms, delivery, and all the other items on the list of things you want up front. Most sales people will try to get your agreement on each item as they go, though, so be prepared to say "maybe" a lot until you get the whole list. What you want to avoid is agreeing to each one individually since you may be able to trade a concession on one for a better offer on the whole package.

Second, don't give up everything you're willing to concede in one large move. You're almost always better off making one small concession at a time. And, as you agree to an item, keep in mind the third point, which is to never make a concession without asking for something in return. In other words, make every offer contingent: "I'll give you this if you give me that." The ideal approach is to offer one concession in return for the entire bundle of things you want from them.

Something else to keep in mind is that negotiation almost always involves some time pressure. You have deadlines such as being nearly out of a something you need for the shop or a customer waiting for a large number of parts to finish a job. The vendor often has time pressure, too, like end-of-month quotas to make or even something as simple as another customer to visit before the day is over. The person with the nearest deadline is most likely to make concessions, so you can use time pressure to your advantage if your deadline falls after the vendor's—or he thinks it does. Making small concessions one at a time helps draw out the negotiations and is more likely to bring time pressures into play.

Time pressure often has a great impact on vendors at trade shows, by the way, because they're often faced with a greater-than-usual number of customers to see in a shorter-than-usual period of time. They also often have special sales goals to meet during the three- or four-day show. The more of his time the vendor has invested in your transaction, the more likely he is to make larger concessions to complete it so he can move on to someone else.

Chapter 9
Training Yourself
"If you want your company to succeed,
you need a business education"

How did you learn your trade? You may have gone to a tech school where such subjects were on the curriculum or you may have picked up the skill informally under the tutelage of a boss or co-worker. It's also possible, of course, that you tackled the task on your own, following an instruction manual or just winging it until you figured out how to get the job done. The point is, you weren't born with that skill, you learned it.

Business skills are acquired the same way. Bookkeeping, marketing, personnel management, negotiation techniques, advertising, forecasting, customer service—they are all skills that a business owner can and should acquire if you want to operate a successful company. As all too many small business operators have found out the hard way, there's more to surviving than learning how to read the printout from a machine tool. Somebody has to run the business side of the business.

Even if you use an accountant, advertising agency, or other specialist to handle all those pesky business details for you, you should know enough about each subject to hire a good professional in the first place, not to mention needing at least a basic grasp of the pro's field so you can monitor their performance and make sure you get what you pay for.

Fortunately, there are all kinds of places where you can sharpen your business skills. You can embark on a self-study program, enroll in a formal college-level course, or get one-on-one coaching from an experienced business owner. As you're looking at the options, remember that, while technical expertise is specialized, business knowledge is not—it's general. The same principles of personnel management apply to a construction company as to a hot rod factory and accounting is accounting, whether it's used in an ice cream parlor or a welding shop.

Local resources

A great place to start is your local chamber of commerce. Give them a call and tell them you want to improve your management skills. They may offer workshops, seminars, or even courses of their own or in conjunction with a college or other organization. At the least, they should be able to direct you to some alternatives.

Your local public library will do the same thing. Libraries these days aren't just places you take your kids on a rainy day. The one in my community has an entire wing specifically devoted to material on how to operate a small business. In addition to shelves full of books on various business skills, there are racks and racks of trade publications, directories, manuals, even videos and DVD's geared to everyone from the rank beginner to the accomplished expert. You may even find The Dynamic Manager Guides on the shelves. Most importantly, there are helpful librarians who will help you find what you're looking for—and the price is right, too.

Of course, you can always go back to school to pick up some useful business knowledge (gee, if I'd only paid attention the first time, right?). If Harvard Business School is beyond your reach, consider a nearby community college or the adult education program offered at your local high school. Most offer a wide variety of courses in everything from advertising and bookkeeping to how to use business-essential software like spreadsheets, databases, and web-publishing tools.

Coaches and trainers

For a more individual approach, there are organizations like SCORE, the Service Corps Of Retired Executives, a volunteer group devoted to helping entrepreneurs start and operate small businesses. SCORE's 10,500 volunteers are working or retired business owners, executives, and corporate leaders who share their wisdom during individual face-to-face confidential counseling sessions and group workshops. Services are free at hundreds of locations throughout the country. SCORE also offers a wealth of useful material online. For more information and to find a chapter near you, go to www.score.org.

Your tax dollars support another service where you can acquire some advice on improving the business side of your shop. The Small Business Administration operates Small Business Development Centers (SBDC's) through a network of colleges and universities, community colleges, vocational schools, chambers of commerce and economic development corporations. They are staffed by volunteers from professional and trade associations, the legal and banking community, academia, chambers of commerce and SCORE (see above). SBDCs also use paid consultants and even consulting engineers from the private sector in some locations to deliver counseling, training and technical assistance in all aspects of small business management. Check it out at www.sba.gov/sbdc.

Many trade associations offer business skills workshops at their shows and expos, at stand-alone events, and even online. Go to their website and click on "Programs & Services," "Education," or "Webinars" to access online audio and videos covering how to do everything from building ad campaigns to designing employee incentive plans. Workshops are often presented by experts in various disciplines including accounting, marketing, and human resources. Many trade groups offer seminars on business management skills at various locations around the country.

Running a successful small business requires two basic sets of skills: technical and managerial. You obviously need to know how to diagnose your customer's problems, which products work best in which applications, and how to install and service them correctly to keep your customer happy. That's the technical side of the operation and most shop owners know they have to constantly update their skills one way or another if they want to keep the customers coming back.

The managerial skills are just as important to your business success. Advertising and marketing brings in customers. Accounting and bookkeeping controls your income and keeps the IRS off your back. Personnel management enables you to hire, train, motivate, and get the most out of your employees. Negotiation skills improve your profit margins. If you want your company to succeed over the long run, you need a business education.

Chapter 10
Case Study: Man Against Machine
"In the electronic world, all the information
is available to everybody right now,"

Technology is a mixed blessing. Just ask anyone who has ever been cut off in the middle of a cell phone call with his mother-in-law. For small business owners, ever-more intrusive digital devices are expanding their capabilities and widening their marketplace while simultaneously threatening to undermine their bottom line.

The bright side of digital technology is the way it speeds diagnostics, improving efficiency so more work can be done in less time. For example, Ray Barney, President of Speed Merchants in San Jose, California, says, "Computer programming for car diagnostics is the most significant technological development" he's seen.

The dark side, though, is the added pressure the computer puts on the mere humans who have to make the computer's pristine, precise data apply to a one-of-a-kind hand-built fuel gobbler that's regularly abused by speed-hungry dirt-trackers, drag-racers, or off-road gonzos. "In the electronic world, all the information is available to everybody right now," says Rob Coverstone, owner of Rob's Speed Shop in Pine Ridge, Arkansas. "Guys with years of experience behind them don't have the edge they used to have."

Coverstone has been in the performance business for forty years. In addition to running a parts business, he and his technicians work on everything from sprint cars to truck pull monsters. He's a big fan of computer diagnostics, but is all too aware of the limitations.

Performance diagnostics

"We can monitor things now that before were trial-and-error and guess-and-by-golly," Coverstone points out. Exhaust gas temperature readings, for example, can tell you there's a problem before it becomes a disaster. "Before, you just blew up a couple of engines and said, 'Something's wrong somewhere.'" These days, you may only have to blow up one engine to fine-tune your settings. "The biggest thing is data acquisition through the computer. You can build or add to a data base, then sort out the information. It spits it out and says 'Hey look, stupid, this is what you're doing.'" Now, variables can be tested in the computer instead of on the dynamometer, making the tuning process much faster which, theoretically at least, means the shop should be able to turn out more work with the same labor.

But have computer diagnostics made the shop more or less profitable? Probably less, according to Coverstone, who points out that, "In the electronic world, all the information is available to everybody right now. Guys with years of experience behind them don't have the edge they used to have."

Not too long ago, he says, "The data used to be strictly hardcore information; a GM head will flow 270 cfm while an aftermarket will flow 300. That doesn't relate to the fact it's a 3300-lb. Camaro and the guy weighs 150 pounds, so 300 is just a little too big.

The computer couldn't decipher that. It had to come from experience." But, as computing power has become cheaper and software more refined, "They're filling those blanks in more and more. Now the computer wants to know the gear ratio, the car weight, whether you intend to run eighth-mile, quarter-mile, or street use. For a long time, that's where we had the advantage: we could read between the lines. Now, the computer is better and better at that."

Management software

Dwight Strobel, owner of Valley Speed Shop in Central City, Nebraska, believes in and uses a great deal of computer technology, too. His fifteen-year-old shop is equipped with sophisticated management software that he also uses to run Strobel Industries, a separate and much larger business that manufactures farm equipment. The program estimates and tracks parts and labor, schedules machine time, and interfaces with the shop's accounting system. The program is a big help, he says, "But you can't anticipate all the issues that are going to come up since every car is a prototype." Besides, "You still have to have the craftsmen to put the parts in and make the thing work." Another problem, as Strobel puts it, is "How do you charge for details" when custom-fabricating and modifying parts?

Ahh, the human factor again. The computer can tell you what to do—most of the time—but it can't do it for you. That creates pressure on the bottom line. As Strobel explains, "The problem is when the part doesn't fit. When you work on a new car, you can use the flat rate manual to figure your time. But there's no manual for street rods. I try to charge for all of our time, but we still probably only get paid for 65% of it. How do you get paid for that other 35%? You just suck it up. I own a piece of every car I ever built."

Online marketing

Yet another way the computer has intruded into the performance shop business, of course, is the ability of customers to shop for parts online. First, some adventuresome bricks-and-mortar retailers showed up on the Internet. Next came aggressive wholesalers and even some manufacturers, who found it hard to resist opening their catalogs to the general public. When Ebay, Amazon, and others made it possible for anybody with a PC to open a storefront web page, the drop-shippers piled on. Where does that leave the local speed shop?

Fortunately, the human factor is at work there, too. "Our customers are definitely online all the time," according to Shirley Kear, owner of Kear's Speed Shop in Tiffin, Ohio. "When they need something, though, nine times out of ten they'll call to talk about it and make sure what they're looking at is what they need." The shop has been in operation for 37 years. In addition to retailing sprint car equipment, Kear has three trucks that sell at area tracks. Her website provides information about the products she sells, her trucks' appearance schedule, and contact information. Someday, she says, she may add online ordering capability.

Coverstone, whose website also displays products information but isn't set up for online transactions, says that, while Internet shopping has its place, "It still always boils down to service. It's not all price." Computers are getting better and better at providing prices, specifications, and even application and installation guidance, but the vast proliferation of information is itself a problem. Search for "cylinder head" on Google, and you'll get over three million results. Refine it by specifying "sprint car cylinder head" and you cut your choices to just under a million.

Perhaps Coverstone's forty years of hands-on experience will come in handy deciphering all that computer-generated data. And who knows, maybe a customer will even pay for it!

Chapter 11
Greening Your Company
"There's more than altruism at work
when businesses sink money into Mother Earth."

Michael Gyory took an old concrete block and steel warehouse in Thornwood, NY, added a third floor while recycling all the steel that was there, insulated it with soy-based spray foam, planted local vegetation to eliminate the need for irrigation, put solar power panels on the roof, and created Thornwood Self Storage Center. Did he and his partner Dan Kasman spend all that money just to be environmentally correct? Not exactly. As Gyory puts it, "We make green by being green."

Ask one of the growing number of county business owners why they're investing in green technology products, and practices, and you won't hear much about melting polar ice caps, carbon footprints, or the endangered yellow-striped wangalooey swimming forlornly up and down the Hudson River. You will get an earful of figures on cost savings, expenses slashed, return on investment, and money in the bank.

Like a growing number of business owners, Gyory found that saving Mother Earth also fattens Father Profit's bank account. He says he could have spent a quarter million dollars less on rehabbing the building using conventional materials and power systems, but he figures they will more than recoup the added cost with reduced operating expenses in the years to come. "People assume— wrongfully—that going green isn't going to make sense economically." Gyory says, then adds, "It's just the opposite."

How much will Gyory save? For starters, his ConEd bill was slashed more than half by the solar panels. "Given current rates, that will be a three- to four-year payout on a twenty-year system," he says. More savings will come from lower natural gas bills due to the insulation and even less electricity being consumed by lighting that is now controlled by motion sensors.

The 82-kilowatt (kW) solar power setup, consisting of 405 Suntech panels installed by Mercury Solar Systems, carried a price tag of $475,000, but thirty percent of the cost was covered by a federal tax credit and the New York State Energy Research and Development Authority (NYSERDA) picked up another thirty percent, so Gyory and Kasman were out only 40%. Gryory admits, "To a great extent, these things only work when there is subsidy money involved."

Starting green

But the point is, they do work—environmentally and economically. And you don't need to build something new from the ground up to take advantage of the possibilities. As Casey Egan, owner of Emma's Ale House in White Plains, NY, puts it, "There's a green alternative to everything from your light bulbs to your computers. And when you're buying new equipment, it's a no-brainer to choose green."

When Egan opened his casual restaurant a few years ago, he didn't set out to operate a green business. By the time he finished, though, he'd installed enough energy-efficient appliances and adopted so many resource-conserving procedures and products that the Green Restaurant Association named Emma's a Certified Green Restaurant, which certifies he meets tough standards for water efficiency, waste reduction, sustainable furnishings and food, energy conservation, handling of disposables, and pollution reduction.

Egan made one small decision after another, using sort of a "save the world one plastic bottle at a time" approach. The single most expensive item he installed was a range that cost about 15% more than an non-green alternative. The appliance uses fuel much more efficiently and cleanly, though. "I'll recoup some of the additional $1,000 on energy savings, but it will take a long time," Egan says. Rather than massively upgrading the central air conditioning system, Egan installed mini-splits, through-the-wall self-contained units that cost more, but can be used more efficiently to cool particular spaces. Energy efficiency is also crucial in a restaurant that has walk-in refrigerators, freezers, and beverage coolers. "You're running them all the time, so they are killers," Egan says. "We replaced three of the four when we moved in. On the other one we put in a new, more efficient compressor."

The little things count, too, according to Egan. "Why anyone would put paper hand towels in a bathroom today is beyond me," he says. "I figure it's around $2,500 a year for hand towels. The electric hand dryers are about $800. And there's no mess!"

And those ubiquitous plastic bottles? "One of the biggest changes we made was in the water we serve," Egan explains. "Instead of selling bottled water, which leaves you with a bottle you have to dispose of, we installed a water dispenser that processes tap water five times and puts it out ice cold. We serve it in glass bottles that we wash and reuse. It cost about $5,000, but at the end of the year, that replaces a lot of plastic bottles."

Ask for a doggie bag for what's left of your Emma Burger (highly apropos since the place is named after Egan's friendly yellow Lab), and you'll get a cost-effective green alternative. "The to-go containers we have are bio-degradable after two years," Egan explains. "We could use one that's made out of corn starch that dissolves immediately, but they're too expensive at this point." He adds, "Some of it is common sense, too. We use bags made from recycled materials, too, but if you're taking home a half sandwich, why do you need a bag as well as a container? It's just going into the trash when you get home."

Major investments

On the other end of the cost spectrum is the extensive greening undergone by the Doral Arrowwood in Purchase, NY—a five-year-old program that will take a million-dollar leap when construction begins on a new 375 kW co-generation heat and power system supplied by American DG Energy. The co-gen system will take excess steam from the Doral's heating plant and convert it into electricity. "We're going to manufacture some of our own power," explains General Manager Steve Mabus. "The technology has come a long way in the last few years."

So has the financing of such projects: "I can't speak too much about the arrangement because of a confidentiality agreement," Mabus says, "but they're going to front the cost of the installation and we'll pay them back over time. That's a creative way to become more green and still manage it from a financial standpoint." As of this writing, they are waiting for town approval to start construction.

Mabus says the Doral looked at solar power as well, but "The system we looked at cost $250,000 and had a ten-year payback. But some of the equipment may have to be replaced at that point, so there wasn't any real savings. You're not sure you're going to derive the amount of savings you estimate, so we're waiting for terms to get better in that area."

Big capital projects aren't the only way the Doral saves by greening its operation. The resort replaced 75% of their lighting with compact fluorescent bulbs and installed motion sensors to turn them off in many areas when not needed. They also replaced six of the eight water heaters on the property with heat exchangers that provide "instant" hot water and installed an organic composter in the kitchen that liquefies waste so it goes into the sewage system rather than a landfill. Mabus adds, "We even outfitted some of our guest service staff with uniforms made out of recycled material to see how comfortable they are. So far, so good. Now we're checking the wear factor before we make a full commitment. There's a lot of neat stuff out there."

The Doral has a green committee that meets once a month. They have a trace list of projects underway and being considered.

Everyone is assigned different areas to research. "Our engineer is looking at capturing condensate from our dryers and recycling it," Mabus says. "He's also looking at other equipment that would enable us to capture waste water and turn it into grey water for use in various places."

Another big spender on green initiatives is C.W. Brown in Armonk, NY, whose $2,000,000 headquarters is the only building (so far) in Westchester County with a Leadership in Energy and Environmental Design (LEED) Platinum Certification by the U.S. Green Building Council. The construction management company earned that honor with major renovations to the building that included a new HVAC system, use of solar tubes to harvest daylight, furniture made from recycled and FSC (Forest Stewardship Council) materials, and a 60kW solar power system.

Smaller businesses get on the green wagon

On the smaller business front, Joseph Curto finds that operating the Yonkers (NY) Indoor Tennis Center with one eye on the bottom line and the other one on the state of the environment makes good senses even if it does cost a little more. The biggest step they took was signing up for ConEd Solution's E-rated Green Power, which certifies that the electricity they use is from 100% environmentally friendly sources like wind and hydropower. "Last year, we spent over $100,000 on electricity," Curto says. " ConEd estimates that our use of Green Power is equivalent to taking a half million car miles off the road." He says it's a couple of cents per kilowatt hour more expensive. "Our bill will probably go up a fraction, but we can justify it in a lot of different ways."

Curto says he looks on greening up as a small marketing expense and adds, "We jumped on environmental initiatives as part of our mission statement to give back to our community." They are also one of the most visible recyclers in the county. "If you walk into a classroom and see tennis balls on the chair legs, you can pretty much bet they came from us." He also says they're starting a program to recycle sneakers. In the end, he says, "We're a small company, but we do a lot of stuff for the community that adds up."

Strauss Paper Company has invested about a half million dollars to go green in the last five years, according to President and co-owner Stewart Strauss. The reason? He says, "If you do your homework, it can be green for the environment and green for your business, too." The latest step they took was to install solar panels on the roof of their warehouse at 3400 Midland in Port Chester, NY. "When you put all the tax benefits and other incentives into the equation, I estimate it will pay for itself in three or four years," he explains. "It's a 20-year life span product."

But that's not the only money-and-earth-saving changes the $50-million company has made. In 2006, they installed an imaging system to replace paper invoices, statements, and proof of delivery forms. "Today, that all goes out by email," Strauss says. "That saves 70,000 pieces of mail, not to mention postage, envelopes, and the gasoline to deliver it." In 2008, the company replaced every light fixture in its 90,000 square foot facility with high efficiency fluorescent lighting. They weren't just taking out standard incandescent bulbs, either. The ones used to light the warehouse were huge mercury vapor domes the size of basketballs. The next year, Strauss installed motion detectors on over 100 lighting fixtures in the warehouse. "There are about thirty aisles in the warehouse that we used to light all day long. Now, if there's nobody in the aisle, there are no lights on," Strauss says. "I figure we reduced our power usage by 25% even before we installed the solar power system." Along the way, they changed all the heating and air conditioning system units—including the boilers—to high efficiency models. Strauss adds, "We even put in a waterless urinal that we're testing now."

Every one of those steps slashes operating expenses while making the world a little cleaner, according to Strauss. One that doesn't is perhaps more symbolic but adds a nice touch of green to employee relations: staffers who buy hybrid cars get a $500 bonus from the company. Strauss says two of his 100 employees have taken him up on it so far.

Bottom line impact

Investing in green technology, facilities, and practices helps reduce expenses, but it's harder to measure the impact on the top line of the income statement, according to just about every business owner I talked to. As Casey Egan put it, "It's not like I'm doing ten percent more business simply because we're not using bottled water. That system is costing me $5,000 more, but it's not bringing in $5,000 more from customers."

Steve Mabus of the Doral agrees. "We pay very close attention to clients and some of our companies ask us for green policies," he says. "I don't know how much difference it makes to them, but we're doing it because it's the right thing to do."

Rich Stitzer, co-owner of catering facility Antun's of Westchester in Elmsford, puts a more positive spin on it. "There are people who want to do business with companies that are green," he says. "We're not 100%, but we're doing as much as we can. We monetize the investment from gaining new customers." Antun's investments started four years ago and have included a $50,000 HVAC system, an upgrade to most of the facilities lighting, and installation of a $20,000 roof membrane that keeps the building both cooler in the summer and warmer in the winter. The company received financing and other assistance from NYSERDA and Public Energy Systems, which supplied compact fluorescent bulbs at reduced cost.

Stitzer says, "We did it for three reasons: to help the environment, save money, and the clients want it." Like most county business owners Antun's went green not just because it's the right thing to do, but because it's the profitable thing to do.

How to Green Your Business

Going green sounds great, but where do you begin? With recycled computer paper? LED office lighting? New heating and air conditioning? Non-toxic cleaning products? No-flush toilets? Hybrid vehicles? A locavore lunchroom? Solar power? There are lots of possibilities, each of which has its own jargon, measurements (what's a lumen, anyway, and how many do you need?), not to mention costs, timelines, tax benefits, and technical ins and outs.

Besides, who has time for all that stuff when you've got a business to run?

Consultant Mark Karell offers some sympathetic advice, "The worst thing to do is just jump in," he says. "First you should determine what you want to accomplish. Do you want to be the greenest company in the county? Or will you be happy somewhere in the middle of the pack. It certainly doesn't make sense to be the leader if it's going to bankrupt you to get there."

Karell is a consulting engineer in Mamaroneck, NY, who has spent the last 20 years providing environmental services to places like the UN headquarters, Jacksonville Airport, and Alberto Culver's plant in Melrose Park, IL.

"It also helps to decide why you're doing this," he adds. "Do you want to save money? Attract more customers? These are perfectly legitimate reasons for going green." He says there are three general areas of concern for a business looking to lower its impact on the environment: electricity, heating fuel, and transportation. "Look at the largest component first—it's usually energy use—and figure out how to reduce its impact on the environment," Karell says. "Or let's say you have a fleet of vehicles. Is it feasible to use hybrids? Or at least better MPG (miles per gallon) vehicles? That's when you look at the economic costs."

You can even get some free or low-cost expert advice during the planning process. Check with your chamber of commerce. Where I live, one good starting point is to sign up for the Westchester Green Business Challenge, a public/private partnership between the County government and the Business Council of

Westchester whose goal is to get all 30,000 businesses in the county to start greening their business with everything from double-sided printing on home office computers to land use policies. Dani Glaser, whose Croton-on-Hudson, NY, company Green Team Spirit administers the program, says it's easy to begin: "The business performs a 20-minute assessment of where they are using one of four scorecards, then sets a plan for greening up."

The process begins when you register online to take the challenge, where you will receive an interactive scorecard outlining up to 82 actions you can take to make your business greener. Not all strategies may apply to your particular company, but the goal is to accomplish as many as you can. As you fill in the scorecard, it links you to targeted resources.

Utilities will help

You can also get help from your local power supplier. In Westchester county, that's ConEd. You'd think the giant utility would want to encourage consumption of more electricity, but they're eager to help customers use less for several reasons, not the least of which is that reducing peak usage saves them money. Regardless of why, you can not only get a free energy audit but some pretty substantial financial help implementing the recommendations. Nearly 900 Westchester companies have taken ConEd up on the offer so far.

A ConEd consultant will come in and do a survey that takes 30 to 90 minutes, according to Esteban Vasquez, Program Manager for the ConEd Small Business Direct Install Program. "We can also provide some equipment for free," Vasquez says. "If they have incandescent bulbs, for example, we'll provide compact fluorescents for free. If they have electric water heating, we can do some upgrades with that. They can start saving energy and money without spending a dime. There's no further obligation, either."

"We offer incentives for other things, too," Valquez continues. "Those can amount to as much as 70% of the cost of some upgrades like upgrading your T12 lighting to T8, installing occupancy sensors, tuning up the air conditioning system and refrigeration." While the business owner can choose their own contractors, ConEd has a cadre of pre-approved vendors available as well. When those are used, the business doesn't have to cover the entire cost of the project and then file for a rebate—they'll be billed only for thirty percent and the contractor will collect the remainder directly from the utility.

Government assistance

NYSERDA, aka the New York State Energy Research and Development Authority, provides a similar service, although surveys and incentives include more than electric-power-related items, according to Westchester Coordinator Elizabeth Sellick. For small businesses using less than $25,000 worth of electricity annually, the audit costs $100. For those whose ConEd bill runs up to $75,000, the fee is $400. "If the customer implements any of the recommended measures, NYSERDA reimburses that fee," Sellick explains. For larger users, the energy study is more comprehensive and NYSERDA does a 50/50 cost share on the study.

For smaller jobs implementing the recommendations, NYSERDA offers cash incentives for HVAC, lighting, refrigeration, and other energy using components from pre-qualified manu-facturers. "All you have to do is send your application with receipts and proof of installation and NYSERDA will send you a check," Sellick says. "For projects qualifying for more than $10,000 worth of incentives, NYSERDA pays based on the number of kilowatt hours reduced by the project. The scope of work has to be pre-approved." Both NYSERDA and the ConEd programs are funded by a little-noticed item on your electric bill, the Systems Benefit Charge, so the business owner can't tap both.

Even green initiatives like installation of solar power systems don't have to be daunting—or prohibitively expensive—but check with your accountant for the full skinny on the costs and returns on investment. Jared Haines, President of Mercury Solar System, points out that solar power costs between $4 and $6 per watt of electricity produced. He says a system will pay for itself in three to five years through lower power bills—savings that will then continue for the expected 25 year life of the system.

C.W. Brown in Armonk, Thornwood Self Storage, and Strauss Paper in Port Chester are among the growing number of business-es (and homeowners) who found the economics—and impact on the environment—attractive. Mercury Solar started in 2006 with four employees in an office in New Rochelle, NY. The company now has eight offices in four states with over 200 employees.

In addition to the power savings, a business can reap the ben-efits of a 30% federal tax credit (at least through 2016) and NYSERDA will fund an additional $1.75 per watt. "If you putt a 10 kW system in, you'll get $17,500," Haines explains. "It usually works out to between another 25 to 35 percent of the cost." And here's where your accountant will be helpful: solar power installations are also entitled to accelerated depreciation, (five vs. thirty years) which produces further tax benefits.

Still not sure you want to go the green route? Consider this point made by consultant Karell: "If you save $100,000 in electricity costs, that's $100,000 added to your bottom line. How much would you have to increase your sales to make $100,000? If your profit margin is 10%, you have to sell $1,000,000 more! And once you change your light bulbs, increase your insulation, or whatever, you reap the savings for years to come. With energy prices constantly rising, so do your savings. Just like the environment is sustainable, these savings are sustainable."

Section Three
Employees

Hiring decisions may be the most important ones a manager makes. Whether adding a salesperson or replacing a clerk, you need to attract qualified candidates, sift through them to choose the best, and hire the individual who will become an asset to the company. While the basic goal of strategic hiring is the same for every business, particular industries often use different tactics to achieve it.

You can't spend too much time or effort on good hiring. The alternative is managing the wrong person for the job, which is far more difficult. A good hire rewards you every day you work with them.

Once they are on staff, people can make or break your business so helping them achieve your goals is key to your company's success. This section covers the entire process from hiring and orienting new employees to training, promoting, and even terminations. Motivation in many forms and dealing with problem employees receive special attention.

Chapter 12

Five Steps to Hiring Good People – An Overview
"You can't spend too much time or effort on good hiring.
The alternative is managing the wrong person for the job,
which is far more difficult."

Hiring decisions are tough because there's so much riding on them—and it's so hard to correct mistakes. A manager can make big decisions about new equipment or product lines or even pricing and then adjust them if they're off track. But when you hire someone who doesn't fit the organization, it's painful to correct your mistakes. So, like the carpenter who learns to measure twice and cut once, you want to make a sound decision in the first place. There are five basic steps to hiring the right person for the job.

1. Define the job
2. Screen applicants
3. Interview candidates
4. Test skills
5. Check references

Define the job

The first step is an internal one. Basically, it boils down to deciding exactly what you want this person to do. What are their responsibilities? That will determine what kinds of skills and experience they need. Will they be interacting with customers? Then they'll need communication skills. Are they going to be building steel structures? It might be useful if they can weld. It sounds obvious, but taking a few minutes to make a list of the things you want your new employee to do will make the whole process easier.

It's tempting to jump ahead and start making a list of qualifications, but unless you have a complete and accurate picture of the specific responsibilities of the job, how can you do that? Take your time and define the tasks to be done first. Then figure out what personal attributes, education or training, and skills the ideal candidate needs to perform those tasks.

You may discover that some skills are essential while others would be simply a bonus. A computer technician may need an intimate knowledge of networking hardware, for example. But one who also speaks Spanish might enable you to open up new markets.

Some skills are better learned on the job, too, particularly if your company has its own way of doing things. Your hair styling salon may be noted for meticulous time-consuming razor cuts, for example, so one of the qualities you'll want in a new employee is an ability to learn to use the specialized instruments used in that process.

Of course, certain jobs require professional licensing or certification, so don't forget to specify them. You may be willing to train a likely candidate, but decide if that's viable before you start hiring.

Screen applicants

The second step in the hiring process, finding candidates to fill a position, isn't easy at all. There are plenty of ways to find people looking for work, but many of them have serious drawbacks. Newspaper help-wanted ads pull applicants who don't know which end of a screwdriver to hold. Trade schools turn out hundreds of eager beavers but their standards may not be as high as yours. Many small businesses rely on word-of-mouth and referrals from current employees, friends, and relatives. The problems that arise with that method come from the personal relationships involved. Did you ever hire your wife's brother? Enough said.

There is no easy solution, but any or all of these methods will bring you some applicants. If you have each one fill out an application and answer a few questions based on the job definition your wrote up (I told you it would come in handy) you can winnow them down pretty quickly. Your goal is just to find a few who meet the minimum standards.

Interviewing

When you have two or three candidates you're seriously considering, sit each one down for an interview. As you do, keep these guidelines in mind:

- Put the candidate at ease at the beginning by asking them questions about their background.

- Ask open-ended questions that encourage the candidate to talk.

- Let the candidate do the talking. You're there to listen and evaluate them…not the other way around. It's a great temptation to slip into selling your company to the candidate. Just remember that they should be doing the selling at this point.

- Before ending the interview, ask the candidate if they have any questions about the job or the company. Keep your answers short and to the point. You're interested in what their questions reveal about them, not about selling them on taking the job.

- Ask the same questions in the same order at every interview. This gives you a basis for comparison between candidates.

- Take light notes during the interview, then write down your impression of the candidate immediately after they leave. Do it NOW while your impressions are fresh.

Remember that the goal of the interview is to form an opinion about the person's drive, their communication skills, their personal ethics, and how they'll get along with the other guys and gals in your company. Their knowledge of your products or services, their mechanical or technical ability, and their experience will influence the ultimate hiring decision, but these can be better determined in other ways at other times than during the job interview. At this stage, you want to know if they are the kind of person you can count on.

Testing

Every job has a set of skills that needs to be mastered. There are technical and mechanical skills, of course (you'll certainly check out an applicant's skills with a production machine before you turn him loose on a million-dollar piece of equipment). But there are others, too, that you might not think about testing—like driving a delivery vehicle. Since you are responsible for an employee's driving while on company business, shouldn't you hire the person with the best driving record?

Other skills are more academic. Can the candidate add and subtract, for example? Even in this day of calculators and computers, just about everyone who works behind a counter should be able to do simple math in their head or on paper. And then, of course, some jobs require advanced or specialized skills like reading a manual or using a computer. In many ways, these are the easiest skills to test since the candidate usually either has the skill or doesn't.

You can't simply ask the candidate if they know how. A good test allows them to demonstrate their skill in some way like taking you for a test drive in your delivery van or working a few simple math problems. Testing isn't hard, but it's an easy step to skip over lightly. Resist that temptation—you'll be glad you did.

References

I'm always surprised when a manager says they've hired someone without checking references. The usual excuse is that the manager assumes the references given by the candidate would only have good things to say, so why bother? These tend to be managers who find out the hard way just how important a background check can be. This is one of those procedures where it's easier to do it right than to undo the damage caused by doing it wrong.

To check backgrounds the right way right, you need to consult three sources:

1. References given
2. People not supplied by the candidate

3. Schools and other organizations the candidate provides.

References can be one of the more difficult things to check. Many companies give defensive answers, confirming only the dates of employment of an individual. Even if that's all you can get from them, it's still valuable information to compare with the dates provided by the candidate on their resume or application. But usually you can learn more by being a little more persistent. Ask the reference for other references. This is one way to check for people not listed by the candidate on the resume.

When you're talking to references and other sources, you'll want to use many of the same techniques you would use during an interview: Ask open-ended questions. Don't telegraph the desired response. Try to keep them talking. Your goal is to gather as much information as you can, so let them do 99% of the talking. It's a good idea to start the conversation with some easy questions. Things like, what job did the candidate have? How many people did he or she work with? How long has the reference known the candidate? These are pretty straight fact-gathering questions that most people wouldn't hesitate to answer.

But you really want to know more than the facts. You want to know about their attitudes and attributes. So ask something like, "If you had to use one word to describe the candidate, what would it be?" You want to hear about the candidate in action, so ask a neutral open-ended question like, "Tell me about their performance." You want to know about their people skills, so ask, "What can you tell me about how they got along with the people they worked with." It's important to find out the candidate's attitude toward work and their employer. One way is to ask about particular behaviors like, "Did they follow instructions?" or "How often did they take initiative?"

And don't overlook the education check. This item is the one most often stretched on a resume or application. It's also not a difficult one to check with a quick phone call to the school district office. Why bother? Because a candidate who lies on their application may lie bout more important things later—like where half of yesterday's cash receipts ended up.

Sleep On It

There's one more thing before you offer that superstar the job—sleep on it. Pausing to reflect is the best way to negate the halo effect, which is where you mentally exaggerate the attributes and qualifications of your final choice. Since you want to choose the right person on their realistic merits, give yourself a little time for a reality check. If you still believe that this is the right person for the job when you wake up in the morning—go ahead and hire them. Just don't be rushed. Hold out for the right person.

You can't spend too much time or effort on good hiring. The alternative is managing the wrong person for the job, which is far more difficult. A good hire rewards you every day you work with them, so focus on the positive steps we've outlined to help you reach that decision. And remember, no matter what recruiting, interviewing, and investigative techniques you've used to evaluate your candidates, nothing takes the place of your own judgment, experience and knowledge of the job.

Chapter 13
Hiring Tips: Wholesale Distributor Sales
"The buyer will ultimately judge
whether you've hired a good salesperson or not."

To find a one-carat gem-quality diamond (which weighs less than 1/100th of an ounce), a mining company sifts through an average of 250 tons of river mud. Sort of like the process you go through to hire a good salesperson.

Hiring a salesperson can be particularly tough because you're looking for someone to represent your company and your lines—to be the public face of your company and to serve as a lynchpin in the relationship between you and your most valuable asset: your customers.

Interviews

"People buy from the salesman, not the company," according to Doyle Harbin, VP Sales, Allison Wholesale of Paint Rock, Alabama. "Personality goes a long way in sales. You've got to be able to get along with people." That single quality—an open, friendly personality—is ranked as most important by nearly every sales manager.

As Robert Canaday, Sales Manager for Buyers Wholesale Distributors, Inc., Indianapolis, says, "I look for personality and a little product knowledge, although they can learn about the products so that's not as important as how well they get along with people."

Fortunately, most sales managers are pretty good at reading people (or they probably wouldn't be in the position in the first place), so judging personality comes almost naturally to them. One caveat, though, is that first impressions aren't always the most accurate. A candidate's true personality shows best when they're relaxed, so good interviews usually start with a few innocuous questions about nothing in particular. "How was traffic coming in?" or "Did you see that game last night?" gets the candidate's mouth working and lets him or her know that you are a human being, too.

A second interview helps, too, because the candidate feels more positive and less threatened with failure if they're called back. Harbin says there are two or three interviews before a decision is reached at Allison, a practice most others confirm.

It's also helpful to take the candidate away from the across-the-desk setting and into a less formal atmosphere. "We walk them around, show them the warehouse, explain what everybody does, and get a feel for their interest," says Ed Karol, VP Sales for Resnick Distributors, New Brunswick, New Jersey.

A relaxed candidate is more likely to be totally honest with you. Karol always asks "Why do you want to be in sales. It's one of the hardest jobs in the world?" Some of the answers would surprise you, he says. "One guy told me he wanted a job where he could be left alone all day. Another one said he liked the idea of working on his own so he could sleep late."

Finally, one of the most important questions in the interview is one the sales manager asks him- or herself. "Was I comfortable with this person?" "Did I enjoy their company?" "Would I want them to call on me?" are some variations of this question that puts the sales manager in the buyer's shoes. The buyer, after all, will ultimately judge whether you've hired a good salesperson or not.

Canaday points out the importance of the human touch: "Even though there's more and more automation in this business, you still need personal service. A Telxon can't tell you they're sorry they sent you the wrong SKU."

Checking References

Karol says Resnick's strict policy is to first verify the driver's license and social security numbers as well as check for a criminal record. Then references are called. Only after these steps are taken do they hold a second interview.

It's also important to find out the candidate's attitude toward work and their employer. "I look first for reliability," Karol says. "Are they dependable? Do they have a track record? We invest a lot in training, so we want someone on board who's going to be here for the long haul." One way to find out is to ask the reference about particular behaviors like, "Did they follow instructions?" or "How often did they take initiative?"

Chapter 14
Hiring Tips: Health Club Staff
"Be patient in your hiring process. You don't have to hire the first person that walks in."

As Yogi Berra might have said, "You gotta be careful about who you interview because you might hire them."

That's the problem faced by health club managers across the country as they look for trainers, sales people, and support staff members who will contribute to the revenue without destroying the bottom line of the club's income statement. It's not an easy process. Finding candidates, interviewing them, and making the hiring decision each present hard-to-solve problems. For example, how much weight do you put on an applicant's work experience during an interview?

"The most important thing is the personality and their demeanor," says Brett Shaw, Assistant General Manager of Lynmar Racquet & Health Club in Colorado Springs, Colorado. "Their experience matters as well," he continues, "but you can have all the experience in the world and, if you don't have a personality, you're not going to last."

Hiring procedures evolve

As the fitness industry consolidates, hiring practices are changing along with many other aspects of club operation. Chris

Lechner, Regional Director of Human Resources for Wellbridge Fitness in Minneapolis, Minnesota, explains that they have moved many of the hiring functions to the corporate level: "What was happening was that the clubs were interviewing and hiring and then the person would be gone within two to three months. We decided that we need to invest more in the recruiting process so we would get more qualified people who would stay and decrease our turnover."

Today, Michelle Kerr, Regional Recruiter for Wellbridge, handles much of the hiring process for management, sales, and trainer positions. "They'll typically apply online, seeing us on one of the job sites or on the local newspaper's website," she explains. "I'll do a phone interview with them and, if they're qualified, I'll bring them in for an in-person interview. From there, I forward them to a club that they may be interested in or live close to. Other positions, mainly hourly positions, will apply right at the club to the manager."

One set of eyeballs on a job candidate isn't enough, according to Lynmar's Shaw. "We do several different interviews," he reports. "One will be with that area's manager, one will be with the club's owner, and, if need be, we'll do a third." Trainers and sales people at Wellbridge also go through at least three interviews, as they do at Landmark.

Wellbridge also tests massage therapists and personal trainers and, according to Lechner, "Group fitness has a practical evaluation," where the applicant auditions their group leadership skills.

Julie Webber, Health Club Manager at the Landmark Racquet & Health Club in Peoria, Illinois, says they're trying out a new evaluation tool: psychological testing. The test takes fifteen to twenty minutes during which the interviewer reads about fifty questions to the applicant. Their answers are sent off to be digitally graded and the results come back within a couple of days. The questions are designed to assess the applicant's dependability, honesty, ability to handle stressful situations, and make sound decisions. Webber says they just started the procedure but she hired the first two people they tested.

Eliminating the hit or miss factor

Personnel decisions may be the most important ones club managers make, so Wellpoint's Kerr observes that it pays to take extra care in evaluating candidates, "Even for the hospitality desk, even though they're the lowest paid employees in the club. They're the ones who have the most contact with the members and they're the ones who can make or break the members' experience with the club."

Lechner agrees that taking extra time and paying extra attention is important. "If they're just hiring warm bodies, they will not be successful," she says. "It comes back to bite them in the end."

Hiring isn't getting any easier, though, because the quality of the work force seems to be declining. "I've been in this business a long time," Lechner says, "and I'd say the work ethic is worse. We have pockets of people who will come in and shine and do a great job, but a high percentage of people just come in to collect a paycheck."

"We're having more people, especially of the younger generation, who aren't willing to put in the hours," Shaw agrees. "Work is more of a have-to than a want-to." He also says there's another problem facing the industry: lax standards. "There are too many people getting certified too easily," he believes. "There needs to be more stringent criteria for getting certified. It's just too easy for someone to take a weight-lifting class in school and call themselves a trainer."

Finding qualified candidates

Help-wanted ads, according to many club managers, are seldom the best place to find candidates for anything other than an entry-level position. Landmark's Webber says: "Sales employees are usually current employees who are promoted from within. We generally do not hire our sales staff off the street because there's so much they need to learn and know about the club prior to that point. They generally come from front desk positions."

She points out another preferred source of employees, club members. "We've hired many members who were qualified," Webber says. "Our current fitness director was a member first, then an instructor, and eventually moved up."

When it comes to finding good trainers, more creative approaches are needed, according to Wellbridge's Kerr. "To attract trainers, we'll do some non-conventional things like mailings and advertising on industry-specific websites or periodicals," Kerr says. "We're also working a lot more with schools that have programs for personal trainers."

Criteria for picking the best

"I look for someone who's enthusiastic and wants to work," Webber says. "The front desk is a busy kind of job where you're on your feet the whole time, you're busy checking members in, so it needs somebody with pretty high energy. I look at whether they're dressed professionally, groomed neatly, because those are things we require."

Shaw takes a particularly close look at his trainer's philosophy: "Eight-five percent of our members are forty-five or older," he says, "so they're looking more to get into shape, tone up. They're not the 'no-pain-no-gain' crowd. That takes a different kind of mentality in a trainer."

Lechner points out another quality to look for in trainers: "Schools don't teach trainers to sell themselves to the members. Even though they may be an excellent trainer, they can't really sell themselves to the members. So we offer internal training in those types of areas to help them build their business more quickly."

When it comes to filling sales positions, Kerr values communications skills more than anything else. "We're looking for someone with a sales background," she says. "We also find people with a communications background whose skills are so strong that they're a good fit for a club sales position. They don't necessarily have to have a hard-core sales background."

Selling the members a good experience means having the right employees to deliver it to them. Webber recommends, "Be patient in your hiring process. You don't have to hire the first person that walks in. I look for quality over quantity."

Chapter 15
Hiring Tips: Automotive Sales
"I look for someone who can engage with the customer."

Auto sales has a notoriously high turnover rate, which makes finding candidates, interviewing them, and making the hiring decision an ongoing process at many dealerships. That doesn't necessarily make it any easier.

Each step in the process raises its own issue. For example, should you hire the applicant who interviews well?

"If the prospect is good at interviewing, it's like a sailor who gets good at bailing; it's probably not a good sign," according to Brian Wolfe, Sales Manager at Pace BMW in Mamaroneck, NY. The professional interviewee, says Wolfe, has read every book and says what he or she knows the interviewer wants to hear. That doesn't make the hiring decision any easier.

Finding qualified candidates

Help-wanted ads, according to many dealers, bring in both the professional interviewee and the car sales "pro" who has an arm-long list of previous jobs. Wolfe says, "We've put ads in the papers, but what you get then are your professional car salespeople who've worked at every dealership under the sun, know who's sleeping with who, who's bad, who's good, and they've got an excuse for every possible thing. They're not personally motivated. They're not self-starters. They're people who need to be managed."

"We've done everything from advertising to word-of-mouth and referrals, and I've found the most success we've had has been through referrals," says Augie Di Feo, President, Chrysler-Jeep of White Plains, NY. Finding good candidates is tough. "I think we as an industry don't draw the best available talent because there's that pre-conceived notion and stigma that this business has created over a number of years," Di Feo continues. "I think experienced people in the next ten or twelve years won't have the same baggage and will come better equipped for the proper way of doing business."

That's why both he and Wolfe, as well as Tim Lynch, General Manager of DeSimone Cadillac Company in Mount Laurel, NJ, don't hesitate to look at candidates without car sales experience. Lynch says they don't have much turnover, but he recalls one instance when "I took one of my best customers who got caught up in a corporate downsizing and made him a salesperson and he did so well that we made him a manager."

Wolfe likes former independent small business owners and has hired several for his seven-person sales staff. "For one reason or another, the business changed or they wanted to sell their business and get into something else where they didn't have to worry about meeting payroll and all of those things," he says. "They're motivated people. They're not clock watchers. You find that type of person and it resonates through their personality."

Qualities to look for

"We believe that the personality fit is more important than anybody's credentials, the skill set, or the experience that they have," says Lynch. "We present our vision, mission, and value statement and ask if they see themselves fitting into our culture. They have to feel comfortable with us, and we have to feel comfortable with them. We are in a people industry, so we look for nice people."

No hustlers need apply, says Lynch. He wants someone who sells smarter, not harder, like one of his first hires, who he observed walked slower than anyone he had ever encountered.. "He said to me, 'I might walk slow, but I write fast.' There's a guy who was thinking," Lynch says. "He's the kind of guy who looks like he's not working hard, but he's methodical, he's constantly thinking, and he's one step ahead of everybody else." Lynch continues, "I hired him and he's been one of my best hires ever. He's been here about eight years now."

"I look for someone who can engage with the customer," Di Feo says. He tells of one engaging young man who came in to interview. "He was putting on a show and he carried a bag of props with him. Inside the bag he had little trinkets that he would use to support whatever he was saying. Like if the customer wanted a little money off on a deal, he'd reach in the bag and throw a handful of monopoly money on the table." Di Feo goes on. "He'd say, 'I'm going to stretch to make this deal,' then he'd pull a rubber band out of his bag and stretch it. He was engaging. He had a world of potential—a very creative mind—but he didn't have any discipline."

Di Feo vets his applicants thoroughly. "First, I get a background check," he says. "What they've done, where they've lived, what type of educational background they have. I try to size up how many jobs they've had over X number of years." He adds that someone else always interviews each candidate as well, and that he never hires someone on the first pass. "I would never hire in a vacuum," he says.

Lynch says he goes even further with his applicants. "They talk to a team of people. Typically, we have them interview with three different people individually. Then we meet to discuss the person to see if we think they are a good fit. Then we bring them back and review them as a panel."

Inside the interview

"If you interview often, you get a taste for what's available," according to Wolfe, who interviews constantly even if he's not trying to fill a current position. He spends as much time as it takes to get to know each candidate, although sometimes, he knows pretty quickly that the person on the other side of the desk isn't going to get hired. "It's not hard to get a lot of information out of them, even bad information. A lot of them will volunteer it easily because they don't think it's negative," Wolfe says.

"I had a person come in from an ad," Wolfe relates. "He was well-dressed, had been in the car business for a while, and was able to tell me about all of my competitors, etc. He must have worked for ten dealers and he was proud as he could be of the list of jobs he'd had. I took the list and asked him why he left each one. The answer each time was that the general manager was 'abusive' or 'hard to work for' or 'couldn't work for them.' We were two minutes into the interview, and I said to myself, do I want to save him some time and turn him down now?"

The process takes time, he says, and that includes time for the applicant to follow up on the interview the same way you'd want him or her to follow up with a prospective buyer. Wolfe tells the story of one young hire: "He was a closer. He was asking me closing questions. He asked me, 'what do I have to do to be employed here?' As much as I hate those kinds of cheesy lines, I knew what he was getting at and I liked it." Wolfe continues, "He followed up with me the next day. He probably left here to go to the post office to dispatch a letter. I then received an email at my home address as well as at my office address, which he had to dig a little to find. He was over the top in that respect." Fewer than half of the applicants he sees use appropriate follow up, according to Wolfe.

In a way, hiring salespeople sounds as simple as following a formula. Find qualified applicants through referrals, conduct multiple in-depth interviews, check the references, observe the applicant's follow-up behavior. Then sleep on it and make a decision. But it's not easy to accomplish all these tasks when you don't have time to do them. All too often, hiring the perfect salesperson just isn't possible because the position needs to be filled—yesterday.

"Sometimes it's like a baseball team; you have to field nine players," observes Di Feo. "They may not be the nine players that you want, but you have to put somebody in every position. Having a poor player with a glove at second base is better than having a hole in your infield."

Wolfe adds that the manager has be adaptable and flexible when hiring. "The interview process is essentially give and take," he says. "Sales is give and take. You don't want to be completely uni-directional."

Chapter 16
Hiring Tips: Craft Gallery Staff
"Measuring someone's work ethic until
you've seen them work is hard. It's a gut thing."

Personnel decisions may be among the most important ones gallery owners and managers make, so most take extra time and care in making a decision. It's a specialized field, so there are some unique aspects to the process like how much weight do you put on an applicant's work experience during an interview?

"We don't count experience very heavily," says Jeanne Kaplan, manager of Artifacts, a gallery in Indianapolis, Indiana. "Retail experience dealing with customers we count, but experience in a gallery we don't because it's so rare to find someone."

Looking for love

What counts more than anything, according to Kaplan and the other gallery owners we interviewed, is a prospective employee's love for the art work featured in the store. Glenn Johnson, owner of the Handworks Gallery of American Crafts in Acton, Massachusetts, says he wants employees who love American craft. "That they're excited about what we carry," is one of his most important criterion, he says, and, "That they're interested and want to learn about it." Johnson likes to hire people with some art background because, he believes, "It makes a big difference in how quickly they come on line and become helpful."

Love for arts and crafts is essential for another, more pragmatic reason, according to Kaplan: "It's difficult finding employees because, for the skills that we need, we can't afford to pay enough. Most of our best employees choose this job for reasons other than the pay. For the flexible schedule or because they like dealing with the pieces we sell. They like speaking with the artists. They like the kinds of customers that we have."

But you can't live on love (so the saying goes), so what else do gallery owners look for? Ruth Lane, co-owner of The Purple Pomegranate in Whitefish, Montana, values reliability and communication skills. "I ask them specific questions about how they would handle a customer," she says. "I'm looking for a very responsible person because they're in here by themselves." She also gives a little math quiz, "so I can be sure they can handle the cash," she adds.

Fishing in the talent pool

Help-wanted ads, according to many gallery owners, are seldom the best place to find the kind of candidates they're looking for. Fortunately, there are simple options. One of the most mundane—sticking a sign in the window—is also one of the best, according to Kaplan because, "people who see it are already interested in the store."

Johnson says, "What's worked for me has been hiring my customers. I've always got a list of a couple of people who are interested, so when it comes time to hire somebody, I just go to that list." In addition, he says, "There are also artists who want to work a couple of days a week because otherwise they're stuck in their studio all the time and they don't get to see people."

Lane faces another hiring problem: The Purple Pomegranate is a seasonal shop, open November through early April for the ski season and again June through September for tourists. She draws on the human resources department of the ski resort where her shop is located for their excess applicants or advertises in the newspaper. She also tried a temporary employment service, but wasn't happy with the quality of employee that came from that experience. "They didn't tell me the employee had to leave to go to school in the middle of the summer season," she explains. Her best luck so far has been in hiring retired or semi-retired part-timers.

Johnson agrees: "Most of my employees are women who are semi-retired. Most of my staff is part time, working two or three days a week, although they work a full day while they're here." Having so many part-timers makes continuity of operations a little more challenging, he says, but the gallery has a well-used employee bulletin board to help communications and organization.

Eliminating the hit or miss factor

Kaplan uses a written application, then puts the applicant through an in-depth interview, usually with both her and her mother, who owns the gallery. "We do call references," she adds. "We've had good information that way."

Johnson doesn't require a written application, but he has a special interview technique to test the applicant's aptitude: "Part of my interview is going around the store and explaining to them some of the processes involved with the specific crafts," he explains. "If their eyes start to glaze over, this probably isn't where they should be. But if they get excited and want to learn more, then they'll impart that to the customers."

As a final step, most gallery owners hire people on a trial basis, as Kaplan says, "For both them and for us. It's hard, because the investment in training is quite a bit." What's more, she adds, "Measuring someone's work ethic until you've actually seen them work is hard. It's a lot of a gut thing."

Chapter 17

Hiring Tips: Sporting Goods Retailers
"It should be a business decision, but a lot of times emotions get in the way."

"Good people are the absolute number one key to everything," says Larry Aasheim, President of Universal Athletic Service, a nine-store sporting goods dealer headquartered in Bozeman, Montana. He adds, "You work hard to find them and it's not easy to do."

Aasheim says they get most of their 200 employees through help-wanted advertising or word-of-mouth, with most openings occurring at the retail store level where strong economies make it tough to compete with jobs in local industry offering $25 per hour. "We have gone to the coaching world to find people," he continues. "We're so involved in athletics, we know a lot of good young people." They often promote promising part timers. Fortunately, he says, they don't have much turnover in the wholesale team operation which accounts for two-thirds of their sales. He has fourteen inside and another fourteen outside salespeople covering four states.

Craig Floyd, owner of Valley Sports in Scotts Valley, California, relies entirely on part time help, most of them high school athletes. He opened the store in at the end of 2003 with six employees and is moving to a new location where the store size--and staff--will more than double. Floyd swears by his young help. "Most of them are quality kids," he points out. "They're high school athletes with high 3.0 grade averages." He says they not only do a good job for him but, "This is a great way for them to have their first or second job doing something they enjoy." He says he has a waiting list of kids wanting jobs in his new store.

Of course, giving young people what might be their first taste of responsibility carries certain risks. Floyd tells the story of one young man: "One of the first days we were open, one of my guys was sitting behind the counter playing a computer game when a customer came in. He looked up and said, 'If you want something, just come and get me.' He actually thought he was being helpful. His brother was working, too, so he came over and punched him in the arm."

After they're hired

Finding good employees isn't the only problem for dealers, according to George Kline, Jr., President of Bethlehem Sporting Goods, which has two retail locations in Bethlehem and Strouds-burg, Pennsylvania. The work ethic has changed over the years, he says, making it a major managerial chore just to keep people moving. Kline, who is the third generation owner of the stores, started working there when he was in the eighth grade and says things were very different. He says, "When I worked for my uncle, you couldn't sit down, you couldn't just stand around. If you weren't working, you had to act like you were working. If we heard his footsteps coming, we jumped to get a rag and started dusting something. We worked for our employer. Now, I feel I work for my employees."

Kids are different today and Kline points out why: "It's us, the parents, that created all those problems. We give them everything that we didn't have. They get the instant gratification of video games and computers; they're not out playing on the corner. We see it in sports! No one's willing to make a decision, to take responsibility. I had a parent call and tell me I sold their son the wrong shorts. I told them to leave him alone and let him grow up—he's in college! It's showing in our workforce."

Dealing with problem employees is no picnic, but Aasheim says they follow a strict set of rules when misbehavior occurs. "We identify the issue, whatever it might be," he explains. We document it and bring them in to discuss it with a couple of people in the room. We write it up, have them sign it, and put it in the file. If it doesn't get better, we bring them in again, write it up again, and put them on probation. If it happens again, they're gone. You have to do it right."

Kline, who says he's sometimes reluctant to pull the trigger because it's tough attracting job applicants. "It should be a business decision, but a lot of times I let my emotions get in the way," he observes. "I say to myself, 'they're nice people.' We accept that they're mediocre and are happy just because they come to work every day. They show up four out of five days, but we don't have any applicants for their job, so we just keep them."

The big No-No

Nearly everyone agrees that worse than mediocrity, though, is employee dishonesty. "It's tough," Klein says. "We're bringing them in as family and trust factors in. You just hate it when that happens to you."

Aasheim agrees. "We've caught people stealing. We have to bring the hammer down on that. They're gone and we make sure people know." He says they automatically forego the "three strikes" rule for employees caught with their hand in the till.

Floyd says he has yet to deal with theft, mainly because his store is so new. He anticipated it, though, and made it clear to his employees what would happen if it became a problem. "I told the employees upfront that the only way I can stay in business is that your friends can't have freebies or discounts and you guys can't take money out of the till. If I go out of business, you guys lose your job," he said.

The care and feeding of employees, be they good, bad, honest, or dishonest, is crucial to every store's success. As Floyd puts it, "The most important is to be upfront with your expectations and the results you expect. Teach them the customer service aspect. If a customer comes in and they're treated well--whether by a fourteen year old kid or a forty year old person—they'll remember that experience and want to come back."

Chapter 18

Make Interviews Meaningful

"The goal of an interview is to listen to the candidate talk."

From the hirer's standpoint, the purpose of the job interview is to learn things that will hopefully predict the potential employee's future success (or failure). Some things I learned while hiring hundreds of salespeople over the years:

- The applicant should do most of the talking. If you spend more time speaking than listening, you're not learning as much about them as they are about you.

- What they say may not be as important as how they say it. Do they speak clearly and convey a positive outlook? Do they get defensive?

- Communication goes both ways, so do they listen well? How much attention they pay to your questions may reveal how much attention they'll pay to those of your customers.

- Appearance isn't everything, but who wants to work with a slob? To find out how neat an applicant really is, go outside and look in their car. If the back seat is full of junk, they may not be as well-kept as they appear.

- Follow-up counts, especially in personal sales. Give the applicant your phone or fax number or your email address, then a day or two to see if they send you a thank-you after the interview.

If they do, it will not only show that they're polite, but that they care enough about the job to go the extra step.

Starter Questions

The goal of an interview is to listen to the candidate talk so you can learn about them. Here are few open-ended questions to start the process:

- Tell me about your work history. Which job did you like best? Why?

- Did you enjoy school? What was your favorite subject? Why?

- Is there anything I should know about your career that doesn't show up on your resume?

- What part of your current (or last) job do you like best? Least?

- Do you like your boss? Why? Why not?

- Describe for me the most difficult problem you've ever faced and tell me how you solved it.

- What do you do best?

- What do you want your employer to do for you?

- Who is the person you most admire? Why?

- Tell me what you do to improve yourself.

Chapter 19
First Things First For New Hires
"A 90-day trial period is common practice
for most small businesses"

A new employee is like someone going on a first date, according to Wayne Price, owner of Superior Auto Restyling. "Everybody combs their hair, ties their shoelaces, and tucks their shirt in so they look pretty," he says. "After a couple of weeks, though, the dirty laundry starts showing up." Price has three locations with about 55 employees in New York.

That's why a 90-day trial period is common practice for most small businesses when they hire someone new. During that time, the company owner has a chance to train and evaluate the employee on several different levels and the employee can size up the situation to see if that's what they really want to do for a living. Usually, the terms of employment during the trial period provide a measure of protection for the shop in case things don't work out. It's a good, solid policy that most business owners swear by.

You can break the 90-day trial period into three phases, although they may overlap depending on how your company operates. First is the orientation, where you acquaint the new hire with the way you do business. Next comes training, which both defines the employee's job and gives them the skills to do it the way you want it done. Finally comes evaluation, when you (and the employee) decide whether your relationship is going to continue and under what terms. Some shops follow strict procedures complete with checklists, forms, manuals, and formal skills tests; others approach the process a little more loosely. The most important thing is to let the employee know what's going on and why so they understand the importance of their performance.

Orientation

Orientation can take a few minutes or a few days. The first thing you need to do is lay out your company's policies on such things as working hours, lunch hours and breaks, sick days, pay schedules, insurance and other benefits, and all the other minutiae of employment—and how all those things will change after the first 90 days. If you have a comprehensive employee manual, great. If not, try to have as much as possible in written form to minimize misunderstandings, especially about pay practices and benefits. Give ample time for plenty of questions to be asked and answered.

Don't just stick to the numbers, either. You should also lay down a few pretty specific guidelines about appearance (hair, clothes, personal hygiene) and conduct (profanity, smoking, cell phone use). You'll want to spell out your business policies—how you deal with customer complaints, returns, credits and exchanges, delivery dates, price negotiation, whatever else matters in the business. It's also useful for the new employee to hear a little company history and to get a feel for how you expect the staff to treat customers, each other, and you.

Training

Some of these things overlap into the training phase. Semantics aside, you can break employee training down into two parts, with differing weights depending on the person's job description. First is product knowledge, particularly important, of course, if your shop sells retail, but also for technicians who may be asked by a customer to compare one product to another. You won't expect a new hire to immediately memorize your inventory or product catalog, but they should at least learn where it is and how to use it. It doesn't hurt for them to know the competitive advantages of your principle lines, too, and what benefits they deliver to the customer. Every employee is a sales person in some way.

The second type of training is skills acquisition. Don't assume the employee knows anything about anything. Even if they've worked in your industry for years, their last employer may have done things completely differently from you. Also, unless you tested their skills as part of the interviewing process, you can't take their word for what they know and what they don't. The best way to teach job skills is to concentrate on process—how the job gets done, step by step—showing them each move, then letting them do it until they get it right before you go on to the next one.

Evaluation

This all leads up to the final phase of the 90-day period: evaluation. The whole point of the process isn't to teach the new hire everything there is to know about your company in three months. It's to see if they have the ability and willingness to learn those things after the trial period is over. You can test their skills and product knowledge. You should also, though, carefully observe them as they go about their duties throughout the period. Do they play well with others? Do they respect the workplace?

Here is a sample check list of questions to ask yourself as you evaluate a new hire:

- Do they listen and follow instructions?
- Do they seek help if needed?
- How well do they accept criticism?
- Do they get along with others?
- Do they have any irritating habits?
- Does their work habits change when unsupervised?
- How do they fill unassigned time?
- Are they eager for more responsibility?
- Do you trust them?
- Do they bring personal problems to work?

As Price points out, "Even beyond knowing if they can do the job, you want to see what happens when they mix with the other employees, if they show up for work on time, do they eat lunch or do something else."

Chapter 20
Making The Good Great
"Few investments have the potential for higher returns than staff training."

Business owners invest in many things: inventory, advertising, shop fixtures, computer systems, even buildings and land. Few investments have the potential for higher returns, however, than those made in staff training. Compared to the average worker, a skilled, educated employee generates more sales, makes fewer costly mistakes, and nurtures greater customer loyalty.

Those skills sometimes come from prior experience, but most good business owners don't count on previous employers to do their training for them. They make it standard practice to invest in their employees by training them, both when they are newly hired and throughout their careers.

The skills covered by most companies fall into three areas: product knowledge, operations, and retail selling techniques.

Product knowledge

"It's very important to us to make sure that our sales staff is very knowledgeable in the crafts that we sell," says Allyson Strowbridge, Marketing Director of The Real Mother Goose, an arts and crafts company which has three Portland, Oregon locations with over 10,000 square feet of retail space and about thirty-five employees. At least 90% of their employees have received some training throughout the course of their career with the gallery, according to Strowbridge.

When a new salesperson is hired, Strowbridge says, "They watch videos, they read quite a lot of written material about the items that we sell, the processes the artists go through, the materials that are used. Videos are informative pieces that we have on the art of glassblowing or various practices with ceramics, for instance." Some artists provide videos, too.

"It's important that the customers know that our employees know what they're talking about," agrees Wendy Dunham, co-owner of Carlyn Galerie in Dallas, Texas, with her mother, Cindi Ray. "We take employees to local shows or glass-blowing studios so they can keep up to date about the artists and how they do their work. It's so much easier to tell the customer when you can appreciate what the artist has done and you know the artist and have a story about them."

Strowbridge adds that the owners of The Real Mother Goose, Stan and Judy Gillis, urge employees to attend trade events as part of their training. "There is money in the budget for some employees to attend conferences and meetings that would add value to their job performance," she says. Local craft fairs and shows are training opportunities, too, she points out, and they offer excellent value because there is usually no cost involved. "Attendance is encouraged because it adds to their knowledge base."

Business operations

In this day when everything from inventory to customer relations is managed through computer systems, it's more important than ever that employees know how to use the digital tools that are the backbone of many business operations. Brenda Leder, owner of By Hand South, a fifteen-year-old art gallery in Decatur, Georgia, says she turned to the consultant who installed their computer's software for employee training. "We did it after work in the evenings," when the system was first installed, she said, "then the consultant was here off and on and we'd all gather around and learn." It's an on-going process, Leder observes, whenever the software is upgraded.

The Real Mother Goose does all operations training at their main location for the sake of uniformity, according to Strowbridge. "We usually have everyone work at our downtown store at least a couple of times before we send them off to another location," she says. "We like to do it that way so people can get familiar with the business end of things."

Sales techniques

Karen Rotenberg, owner of Alianza Contemporary Crafts in Boston, Massachusetts, emphasizes professional customer relations when training a new employee for her 1,200 square-foot gallery. Working with the gallery manager, she says, "the new people observe carefully how customers are handled, how they are treated, and how the work is presented to the customer. Some of this you can tell the person about, but if they can observe it done in ways that are successful and meaningful to the work, I've always found that's the best way."

There are many lessons the employee hopefully learns this way, Rotenberg says: "One thing that should be taught to every salesperson is that every customer should be greeted and made to feel comfortable" when they enter the gallery. "Then there is the issue of over-servicing the customer and not giving them the opportunity to look around and observe the works on the own. You need to maintain a balance between providing enough information and not too much."

"We usually have a new hire shadow one of the sales people," Strowbridge agrees, although she says The Real Mother Goose assumes they have selling skills already since most new hires have some retail sales experience when they are hired.

When it comes to selling skills, none of the galleries we talked to bring in any outside help to train employees, relying instead on managers and experienced staff members to convey their knowledge to other members of the staff. "When you have somebody that's worked for you for a long period of time, they become the ultimate trainer," says Rotenberg.

"The other thing that's very important is to listen to the customer," Rotenberg adds. "As much as you try to inform them, they can inform you, too."

Employees aren't the only ones who can benefit from a learning experience, either. As Wendy Dunham says, "We represent over 400 artists, and it's one of those things where, every single day, employees are learning new things. I'm learning things every day as well."

Regardless of how it's done, whether employees study literature and videos supplied by the company's suppliers, take computer lessons supplied by a vendor, or shadow and observe experienced employees, most business owners would agree that the time and money spent on staff training is an investment that pays off in the long term.

Home-grown training

Hiring professional trainers or sending staff members to specialized courses can be prohibitively expensive. That's why small businesses often handle most of their training in-house.

Here are some guidelines to make do-it-yourself staff training more effective, according to Dr. Arnie Witchel of the University of Phoenix (Orlando Campus):

- Outline the skills or knowledge base you want to cover before you begin.

- Divide the subject into "bite-size" lessons and give the employee time to absorb one before the next one is presented.

- If possible, have some written material (or other media) the employee can study and refer to later.

- People learn best by doing, not by listening or observing, so have them practice the skill whenever you can.

- Accountability counts! A simple quiz at the end of each lesson improves attention and encourages retention.

Like many other processes, preparation for training takes time but improves the end result immensely. Once the outline, materials, exercises, and quizzes are ready, though, they can be used repeatedly for the next new employee you hire.

Chapter 21

Should You Bribe Or Bully?

"Negative motivation is probably a contradiction in terms."

Running a small business is like driving a race car: you can conceivably do it all by yourself but your odds of winning are better if you've got a motivated team working for you in the pits. That team of delivery truck drivers, bookkeepers, service personnel, technicians, and salespeople is essential to keeping your business operating at top speed. But as any NASCAR driver will tell you, it isn't how many warm bodies you have standing around in the pits, it's how motivated they are to put out some extra effort that makes the difference between finishing first or last.

Most small business owners will agree that employee motivation begins with the hiring process. If you hire good people in the first place, half the battle is won. "You always have the problem of finding good people," according to LP gas dealer Eldon Bultman of LPG Delivery Service in Elkhart, Kansas.

John Holloway, owner of Tri-State Propane in Hiwasse, Arkansas, says he tries to hire known quantities: "I've lived in this area my whole life, so I mainly hire people I know personally," he says. "I try to hire the type of person that I know is safe and easy to get along with." Holloway has ten employees. "I look for good people people," he adds. "I sit down and have a personal interview and try to get a feel for how they're going to associate with the customer and how they feel about safety and we have a pretty thorough interview." Holloway also runs thorough background checks and contacts references.

Once they're on the team, the next step in motivating the employee is making sure they understand what's expected of them. "I just sit down and talk to them about what the job entails," Bultman notes. "I tell them what they're expected to do and what time I expect them to be here. How many hours they have to work. Then I go over the work they're going to be doing."

Constant feedback during the crucial first few weeks on the job helps, too, according to Laurie Gore, who owns and operates Mountain Propane in Port Hadlock, Washington, with her husband Rick. She says they give the new employee a flexible period to prove themselves on the job: "Some people learn faster or slower than others. Usually, by the time sixty days is hitting close, we know whether they're going to make it or not."

Long-haul motivation

After the probation period ends, though, the fun begins as you and the no-longer-new employee settle down to the daily grind of business. Sometimes, it seems, the employee's main goal is to see just how little effort needs to be expended to earn a day's pay. Most company owners will agree that it's not the employee who grossly misbehaves that presents the biggest problem, it's the one who performs at maybe sixty percent of their potential day after day that saps profitability. The bad character draws attention to himself and can be terminated; the under-performer hides in the weeds. "It's when they stand around waiting for someone to tell them what to do that I don't appreciate it, especially when there are obvious things that need to be done," says Gore.

Generational differences are sometimes the culprit, according to Bultman. "Normally speaking, the older workers value their job a little bit more than the young ones," he says. "It's a trend of the times. A lot of the young ones figure that if they lose this job they'll just find another one."

Gore agrees, saying, "Older employees have better work ethics because the younger ones seem to expect things handed to them for nothing. The older people know they have to work for it or they won't get it."

One way to face this problem head-on and keep productivity up is to constantly reiterate what needs to be done and who on the staff is supposed to do it. It's important to recognize each individual's state of mind, though. Holloway does this during daily meetings. "We all talk," he says. "We have a meeting every morning in the driver's room. I can get a feel if they're not feeling good that day or got into it with their wife and are mad at the world."

Gore stresses interpersonal communication, too. "We have some written policies to cover the basics, but we try to keep open communications and do things verbally on a constant basis," she says. She reports that they have regular staff meetings during the summer when there's time, but handles communications one-on-one during the hectic winter months.

Another positive motivator is the example set by the boss, at least according to Holloway. Working side by side with the employees every day serves another important purpose, too. "Since I work hand in hand and go out with them, I see how they're working," he points out. "We haul gas and set tanks together. I get in there and dig ditches with them. If they see me doing it, they know what they're supposed to be doing."

Short-term approaches

Negative motivation is probably a contradiction in terms, as anyone with teenage children has observed. Punishment such as docked wages or a probationary period may temporarily stop the offender who is grossly negligent, blatantly dishonest, or rudely intransigent, but the change in behavior is seldom permanent. About the best that can be done is to clearly communicate your desires and the consequences of further misbehavior. "We look at each person as an individual," says Gore. "If somebody starts out not doing very well and we give them more instruction and more feedback and they improve, we'll keep them. If they keep doing the same thing over and over again after they've been instructed two or three times, then we usually let them go."

"We just sit down and have a talk," Bultman agrees. "I tell them this is what they have to do." He points out, though, that there are downsides to termination: "I usually hesitate about firing them because the first thing they're going to do is file for unemployment. They love that."

The ultimate motivation tool, nearly everyone agrees, is a stack of documents signed by the Treasurer of the United States. Money works well as a reward on both a long-term and short-term basis. Bultman doesn't pay any bonuses, for example, but is more than willing to give raises to employees whose performance brings in new customers or otherwise contributes to the company's bottom line. Gore says that her employees who perform above and beyond the call of duty are given cash bonuses.

Holloway likes to hand out one-time rewards, too. "If we pick up a new customer, I try to give the driver a bonus," he reports, although he believes they work to sign up new accounts for another reason as well. "They like to see us grow and do well, too," he says. "That's just job stability for them. The money doesn't hurt anything."

Chapter 22
Fire 'Em Up Or Just Fire 'Em?
"How do you get employees to do what you want them to do?

"If I didn't have to deal with customers and employees, running a shop would be easy," goes the old saw about business management. Putting customers aside for another day, let's deal with the employee situation for a moment. Specifically, how do you get them to do what you want them to do?

"To begin with, we make sure that we hire good, skilled people that are interested in making money for themselves," says Shelly Plekowski, who runs Suburban Rod and Custom Classics in Merriam, Kansas, with her husband Jim. "When the body man or the painter is making money, that means the shop is making money." Jim and Shelly bought the long-established shop near Kansas City in 1992. They do body work, mechanical, and interiors in a 12,000 square foot shop with ten full time and a handful of part timers.

Steve Hemstock, who owns Knights Autoworks in West Allis, Wisconsin, agrees that having a motivated employee starts with hiring the right person in the first place. He says, "It takes something that's in a person before you hire them to make a good trimmer." Hemstock has been in business for three years for himself, but comes from a long line of upholsterers. He was also a general manager for Classic Soft Trim and estimates he has supervised a hundred men over the years.

Many small business owners look first at the potential employee's skills and knowledge as reflected by their years of experience on the job. While it's important to know that the person is capable of doing the work, what may be even more essential is their willingness to do it up to your company standards—all the time. That's why Hemstock says, "I'm basically looking for somebody that has the desire to get ahead. I'll teach them the trade." He continues, "I don't need experience. What I do need is the core talent." They'll get experience on the job, according to him: "You can teach anybody to be a seat cover guy. I've taught three guys who didn't even speak English how to sew."

Plekowski agrees. She says, "It's difficult to find good body men. What we try to do is find young guys that want to learn and are willing to start out like an apprentice."

Once they are hired, how do you get the performance you need to operate a profitable shop? Bobby Mass, owner of Automotive Restyling Masters in Laurel, Maryland, has been in business for six years and has not had a great deal of success with employees. "What's been lacking is the ability to do it right the first time," he says. "I can understand a mistake here and there and you learn by doing, but I've found a lot of people don't have common sense."

In praise of praise

For Plekowski, it's a pretty straightforward proposition: "We don't really have a motivation program per se other than you do good work, you have good skills, you have good work habits or you don't work here."

Suburban Rod and Custom has two distinct sides to their shop: collision repair and what they call the hot rod shop, where custom show-quality cars are built and restored. Plekowski says they don't have any trouble at all with motivating the guys in the hot rod shop. "They are artists and they take a lot of pride in what they do," she says. "They enjoy knowing that, when we're finished with a car, it's an award-winner. A lot of the cars we build are shown and they win awards and our guys like knowing that."

Those men had the will to do quality work when they were hired, she believes. "The motivation for the guys in the hot rod shop is their own ego and their own sense of personal satisfaction," she adds. "When they're finished with the job and they see the end result, that's enough motivation for some of them in itself. They enjoy the money they make, but there is that ego involved."

"It's a shared sense of pride when we're finished with these cars and the vehicle owner is just tickled to death," Plekowski says. "The guys that built the car are just as pleased as he is. There's nothing more satisfying than to have a customer that's just so tickled when you're finished that he's grinning like an idiot."

As someone once put it, praise does wonder for a sense of hearing. We think of motivation as something you do to salespeople or assembly-line workers. Do more! Sell more! Make more! But every employee (and partner, co-worker, or spouse, for that matter) needs a little shot in the arm every once in a while to help them get through the day and do what needs to be done to make your business run better. As Plekowski says, "You appreciate your own work, but when somebody else appreciates it and brags on it and compliments you on it, you get a huge boost to your ego."

People will be human

But, as Vincent Van Gogh's mother knew all too well, artists can be temperamental. What do you do with the guy who has an attitude problem? Hemstock says simply, "Leave him alone. If you try to mold him and reform him and tell him 'you have to be this and that', you're going against his grain. Why would you do that to a fellow?"

"Don't let him talk to customers, if you can, to start with," he elaborates. "Listen to what he tells you because he may not understand all the business end of things, but he understands the production end of things. If a guy doesn't get along with society, don't put him in society."

Hemstock values the employee who thinks outside the box and puts some heart and soul into his work, but he understands their limitations, too. Sometimes, they're loners, which presents its own set of problems. His solution? "If a guy doesn't get along with two other guys in the shop, then give him his own things to do," he says. "Give him an environment where he can thrive, and he will excel."

Sometimes, of course, it just doesn't work out and the relationship sours. Plekowski says they can't afford too many mistakes or employee problems: "In a shop like ours, there's very little leeway for someone who does sloppy work or has poor attendance. Our main number one job here is customer service. That's doing a proper repair with good quality work and getting it done as quickly and as efficiently as possible."

Mass let someone go just recently, which is a managerial task familiar to every shop owner. The problem? "I had to work around his hours. His work was great, but I couldn't deal with working around his hours. We weren't on the same page."

In a way, customer relationships are easy: you do good work, they pay you, and everybody's happy. It's the employee relationships that are hard. Marshaling the right people to work well isn't a one-time event. It's the day-after-day, hour-by-hour job description of small business management.

Chapter 23
Case Study: Retail Employee Motivation De-Mystified
"Every employee is different and
needs to be treated accordingly."

To motivate an employee is to get them to act in a certain way; to persuade them to do what you want them to do. Any retail shop owner who has ever watched an employee answer their cellphone while they ignore a customer knows this is easier said than done.

There is no one key to employee motivation. While some managers swear by compensation plans that reward good performance, others rely instead on clear rules of conduct and a firm hand to enforce them. There are those who admonish and those who coach. Some cajole while others lecture. Almost every small business owner agrees that no one approach motivates best.

Linda Branch works with twelve employees at The Courtyard Gallery, her 6,000-square foot shop in Lindsborg, KS. She says a good manager has to take the lead by setting priorities, providing a positive work environment, and giving clear, encouraging instructions. She also believes every employee is different and needs to be treated accordingly. "If we're slow, one person will jump in and start cleaning while another one will pull out a book and start reading," she says. "Some get it more than others."

Her employees range from high school kids that work in the coffee-shop and bakery that's part of the gallery to a computer-savvy farmer's wife who manages the inventory and website. "There are times, especially with the younger ones, you have to jump in and be a mother to them," she explains. "You have to re-mind that that this has to be done and that has to be done."

"I hardly ever use the words 'no' or 'don't' or 'you didn't' or anything negative like that," she adds. Branch says she learned that approach from training she received in her corporate position be-fore she opened the gallery. "You talk about the wonderful things they are doing, then you say 'I prefer things done this way. Let's work on this.'"

Does money motivate?

Motivation is equated to compensation by managers in many industries, but gallery owners don't typically place much emphasis on it. Mary Benjamin, one of five artists who own Bluestem Mis-souri Crafts in Columbia, Missouri, reports that their employees are paid an hourly wage and a bonus during the holidays. "Essentially, they're working for the love of the art, not for money," she says, although they also receive discounts on works from the gallery.

Richard Herrmann, who owns the Ironwood Gallery in Ridgewood, Connecticut, with partner Betsy Halliday, agrees. "We don't offer a commission" to their two employees, he says. "We pay them hourly and offer them a very appropriate discount on work in the gallery. In a sense, that's motivating."

Branch rewards employees for exemplary performance spon-taneously, using monetary compensation to motivate in an almost symbolic way. "If I get a nice compliment about someone on the staff," she explains, "I'll take five dollars and give it to them and say 'great job!' It's not the size of the reward, it's the recognition." The positive message carries throughout the gallery: "It affects the other folks, too."

Motivating talented people

The environment where people work, the way they are treated, even the tasks they are given to carry out can either motivate or de-motivate a company's employees. Herrmann feels it's important to have both realistic expectations of employees and to make sure their job description matches their skills. The gallery has two part timers on staff, both of whom are working artists. "I understand what they're good at and what they're not good at," he says. Once a sale is made, for example, all they have to do is write up a ticket for the item and the sales tax and run the credit card. "I don't have them enter it into the computer system," he explains. "It's enough that they know the alarm code."

Some gallery owners find that artists don't make strong sales people, but Herrmann looks at it differently. "Even if the people who work for us aren't necessarily the best salespeople in terms of techniques, they're certainly ingenuous and forward," he says. Their knowledge of the art-making process makes them uniquely qualified to represent it to customers, which more than compensates for other shortcomings they might have: "They're not sales-motivated. They're not going to leap on a customer. They're going to talk about the work from an artist's perspective. Our clients like that."

Benjamin agrees, saying that allowing Bluestem's four employees to use their talents helps both them and the gallery. "We have somebody right now who used to curate documents for the University of Missouri. She's brilliant with computer and writing skills," she points out. "We have another person who used to do displays for a major department store and she brings us ideas. We let people grow into an area where they feel strong and are able to do the work."

Seemingly simple things like the hours they work can have a huge impact on people's attitudes. Branch explains her approach by saying, "We try hard to make it so that people aren't giving up their life to work here." She meets with her entire staff monthly to work out the schedule.

Erica Hume manages two employees for Artwood, an eighteen-year-old gallery in Bellingham, Washington, and agrees wholeheartedly with Branch. "We're very flexible in our days off," she says. "They have children; they have grandchildren, they want to visit and we work it out."

Motivational gurus will argue that the best way to motivate someone is to help them attain something they want, whether it's more money, more time with their kids, or more personal growth, if they'll do what you want in turn, such as treating customers like royalty, learning the stories behind the artists you represent, or just straightening the stockroom during slow times. Most small business owners say it also helps to hire people who have a good work ethic to start with. Hume says that quality describes her staff: "If dusting needs to be done, they do it. If there's a leak, they put a bucket under it. They just do what needs to be done."

Keeping your staff motivated pays off in several ways, according to Branch. "It is so much easier to work with people and get them to where you want them than it is to constantly hire and train more," she says. "I hate that. Every time you start again, you're behind."

Chapter 24
Case Study: Tune Up Your Technicians
"It's essential that the technicians be motivated
to do the job right the first time."

If you're in the automotive service business, odds are good that you know how to make an engine produce more power and a transmission how to operate more efficiently. From a management standpoint, though, do you know how to do the same thing with your employees? A stint on the dyno and a little tweaking of the fuel mixture can motivate an engine to perform better, but what motivates a technician?

Some shop owners swear by the stick while others are firmly committed to the carrot. Some believe in incentive pay and formal year-end bonuses while others will tell you that the best employees are those who work for the love of fast cars and the pure joy that comes from smelling rubber burn. Nearly all will agree, though, that having motivated employees is critical to a shop's success.

John Boos is a road racer who owns a shop with three employees in Anoka, Minnesota. Boos Performance specializes in Corvette, Camaro, and Firebird modification, repair, and restoration. He's been in the performance business for twenty years and says, "The single most important thing in my business has been finding good employees. It's also been the most difficult thing."

Why? "Because all my customers belong to clubs; I can't have mistakes coming back on me. Unlike general auto repair, everything has to leave here right." That makes employees who can produce solid, dependable work essential to the success of the business.

That's one of the unique motivational challenges of the automotive service business. In many industries the goal is to produce more work faster. Quality is important, but it often takes a back seat to quantity. In an automotive performance shop, it's essential that the technicians be motivated to do the job right the first time. "It takes a unique individual who pays attention to detail," Boos says. "He has to understand things like the importance of not leaning a broom against the car. A twenty-year GM tech doesn't do me any good if I'm repainting a car every other day."

Pande Talevski, owner of Pande's Performance in Livonia, Michigan, addresses that situation in the hiring process. He's run his full-service race shop for nine years and has four employees. "I like to get them when they don't have habits already so they can fall into the habits of the way we work." He invests a lot of time training his employees to work the way he wants them to, which presents a motivational problem in and of itself—you have to make them want to learn—but also serves as a motivational tool because most people appreciate a boss who will take the time to help them improve their performance.

In addition, Talevski ties annual raises loosely to employee skill levels. "The more you learn, the more I give you," he tells them. The economics are simple: the more an employee knows, the more valuable he is to the shop.

Boos agrees, and adds, "I'd rather teach a smart person who has never worked in a shop but is organized and detail oriented how to do this than try to teach a mechanic slob coming out of a high-volume shop how to be a clean technician in this kind of place. Here, you've got to go fast, but you've got to dot your 'i's and cross your 't's first."

Keep those spirits up

When it comes to output and level of performance, "We have our good days and our bad days," Talevski says. "Certain days, it seems like we'll get a ton of stuff done. Others, it seems like we're working our butts off but can't get ahead. I think at certain times, you just get burned out."

One of the motivational problems shop owners face constantly, according to Talevski, is the pressure from customers who demand instant gratification. "All the people we deal with in this industry are like children. They have to have it right now. That kind of wears on the employees when they hear the customer whining. The employee can get kind of discouraged."

What's his solution? "I try to give them some breathing room. I tell them not to worry about it. I'd rather they take their time and do it right, rather than hurry up and get it done and then have it come back later because there's a problem."

Talevski also takes the time to make sure his technicians feel like they're part of the team running the business, not just flunkies doing the grunt work the boss doesn't want to do.

"Sometimes we butt heads if they think they have a better idea than what we've already been doing, but we talk about it," he says.

"We put it on the table. If I feel it's better, I don't mind changing. Just because I own the place doesn't mean I'm always right." That willingness to listen makes the employees feel valued, which in turn makes them want to live up to their position. An employee who is treated like an interchangeable cog in a machine generally works only as hard as they're pushed. One who believes he's an important member of the team will feel obligated to contribute to its success. The key factor is the amount of communication. "I make the final decision, but I don't do that until everybody agrees on it."

Show me the money

Talk to ten managers about the importance of money when it comes to producing performance and you'll get ten different answers. Still, everybody needs a basic living wage and there are few people in any industry who don't feel that superior workers deserve superior compensation. The rub comes when you try to tie pay to performance in a quality-oriented business like an automotive repair shop.

Boos relies on the flat rate system to compensate his technicians. "We pay a base salary guarantee against a generous portion of the flat rate." Because of the nature of the work, Boos says, his flat rate is considerably higher than most shops in the area, which also allows him to reward his technicians for their efficiency.

Talevski doesn't provide any formal incentive pay or bonuses, but makes a point to periodically review wages and pass out raises when warranted. He also tries to keep an ear open to opportunities to reward good employees in ways that meet their particular situations. "If my employees need something, I do the best I can to take care of them." If a technician wants to work on his own car, Talev-ski provides his own knowledge and labor at no charge. He'll also help an employee finance expensive parts by paying for them through payroll deduction.

Boos practices creative compensation, too. "Last year, I gave a guy a Corvette," he says. "It had a blown engine in it, but it sure beats a ham." The employee was carrying a big load in the shop and Boos felt he should be rewarded in some way. "With his family and everything else, he wasn't able to afford one himself. I had the car and it just worked out."

You can't please all the people all the time, though, and not every employee is going to respond to your motivational efforts. Some people just seem to have been born with a cloud over their heads and the ability to put everyone else in the shop under its shadow. Talevski had someone like that a couple of years ago, he says: "He was one of those guys who kind of depressed everybody in the shop. That was probably the worst time I've had." The solution? Remove the problem at the source. "You let them go, cut your losses and move on," he advises.

In many ways, motivating a vehicle to work better is easy: slap on an afterburner and crank 'er up. Motivating your employees to work better, though, requires a lot more thought, patience, and creativity.

Chapter 25

Solving The Problem Of Problem Employees
"Employees are human and business owners
have to deal with that."

Employee problems? "That's the icky part about being the owner of your own business," according to Stephanie Fleishman, who runs gallery 2910 on the Square in Canton, Maryland. She sums up the feelings of many small business owners who are faced with an undeniable fact: no employee is perfect.

They make mistakes. They wake up on the wrong side of the bed and make things uncomfortable for everyone in the shop. They forget things, like showing up for work. In short, employees are human and business owners have to deal with that fact. As Fleishman says, "Trying to manage people isn't always easy."

Specialty shop employees may actually present some unique problems due to the very nature of the trade. For one thing, their bosses are usually in the business because they love their niche— and they often hope to hire employees who feel the same way. As Scott Robertson, owner with his wife Pat of Arrivee Gallery in Long Branch, New Jersey, points out, "Everybody is passionate for what they do because we're all passionate for the art." In his gallery, he says, "There are no motivation issues."

Unrealistic expectations

But, as Monica Maxwell, who owns Harmony Ridge Gallery with her husband Aaron in Lewisburg, West Virginia explains, some employees are seduced by the relaxed ambiance many galleries try to create for their customers. "When someone first comes in and applies for a job in a gallery, it seems like it's a nice, simple, pleasant place where you don't really have to work too hard. The atmosphere sometimes gives people that vibe." But then they discover that it's a job of work, as they say in Scotland. Gallery employees are expected to be much more knowledgeable about the merchandise they sell than the average retail clerk at the Gap: "When the reality kicks in that there is a certain way to sell and there are very specific ways we do things" that they have to follow, "that's a little overwhelming for some people," she says.

On the other hand, the nature of the specialty retail business helps the manager, too, since many shop owners spend a lot of time on the floor, where they can watch what their employees are doing. As Maxwell says, "We observe what they might say about something, how they might approach someone, how they might be gift wrapping." The advantage? "There are constant little tweaks that you make with them because you yourself are always learning new ways to say things or do things." Since you're not asking the employee to do something you yourself won't do, the suggestions are usually better received.

"We don't have the traditional problems because no one is working for anyone else, we're all working together," says Robertson. "If everybody knows that their voice will be heard, that's where you start. Then you treat each other with respect and it goes a long way." He adds, "There are no manuals. It's all common sense and respect and social skills."

Hiring the right people in the first place helps, of course. As Maxwell says, "Personality is key when we interview someone. Even if they have great qualifications, if we don't click, we look for someone else." That's especially important in intimate workplaces like most specialty shops. Making job responsibilities clear when an employee is first hired, or when their job changes, is another key to eliminating problems before they arise. It's remarkable how much better people perform when they know what they're supposed to do and how they're supposed to do it.

Employee communication keys

Here are five principles that will help you communicate effectively about employee behavior:

1. Act immediately. If you spot a problem, raise the issue as soon as practical so it doesn't fester.

2. Determine why. You'll approach a problem rooted in ignorance differently from one that stems from poor attitude.

3. Be specific. Be clear about what you want done, when you want it done, and who you want to do it.

4. Explain why. You don't need to justify your decisions, but the employee will be more amenable to change if they understand the reasons behind it.

5. Get agreement. Even if they don't like it, the employee needs to agree to change their behavior or you're going to face the same problem later.

Everyone is different

When problems do arise, the way the manager brings up issues makes a difference. How you should approach each person depends on the individual, according to Maxwell: "Some people are more sensitive and they might take it as a negative criticism. Others are totally open to hearing how they can do things better. In general, we make it a very casual remark." She says things like "I noticed how you gift-wrapped that item. It might be a good idea to do it this way next time," or, "I noticed that when you were talking about that glass piece in the window, you might also want to mention blah-blah-blah."

Timing matters, too. "We make it a point to say those things afterward," Maxwell adds. "Let the whole sales experience happen, and then share the information. We don't wait too long, though, since we want it to be still fresh."

So what do you do if the casual approach doesn't achieve the desired result? What if the employee doesn't pay attention, doesn't understand your instructions, or just doesn't care? Maxwell starts by getting the employee's full attention and getting to the bottom of the problem. She explains, "We go into the office and sit down. I say, 'this concerns me. I've pointed it out a couple of times. Is there a reason you're not doing it?' I make it a point to say this is an important part of your job."

Terminal decision

And then? "By the second time, if we have to call them aside again, we're at the point where we have to say, 'either fix this or else.' There is a kind of three-strikes-and-you're out," according to Maxwell.

It should be standard operating procedure to put a written record of all such conversations into the employee's file, no matter how informal they might be. People change; good situations turn bad and, regrettably, you never know when you're going to have to defend yourself and your business legally. Maxwell explains their policy: "Even if it's a casual conversation, we put a note in there. If it's a serious conversation, we ask them to sign the note. You always want to have a track record. Like anything else you do in your business, documentation is extremely important."

Termination is never easy, but it can be a positive solution. Fleishman struggled with a problem employee for two years, a woman who "made it difficult to work with the other employees." When she let the woman go, Fleishman says, "I was in tears when I exited the interview," but later she felt like a weight had been lifted off her shoulders.

Chapter 26

Do You Need A Second-in-Command?

"Choosing the right person for the job is a critical decision."

There comes a time in every company's growth cycle when it needs a supervisor of some sort in addition to the owner. You might need a shop manager to schedule the work flow while you deal with customers and vendors, a sales manager to run the retail operation while you oversees the shop staff, or even a general manager to manage the day-to-day business while you handle finances, marketing, and the myriad other details that come along with running a mid-size business. Whatever the duties of your company's middle managers, choosing the right person for the job is a critical decision. Training and managing the managers is important, too.

When you decide it's time to add a layer of management to your shop, there are two places to find the right person: from the ranks of current employees or from outside, usually from a competitor or similar business. Each path has its advantages and disadvantages, but some of the basic principles are identical.

The first step in hiring a good manager is taken long before you start interviewing candidates for the job. Before you do anything else, you should develop an accurate, detailed job description for the position. It needs to cover the specifics of what you expect the manager to do, exactly what their responsibilities are, how much authority they have, and how they are going to be evaluated. Some items to consider include:

- Which specific functions do they oversee?
- Which employees report to them and which ones don't?
- Can they hire, fire, discipline, or reward the people who report to them?
- Are they expected to perform shop work as well as supervise others?
- Can they authorize spending for inventory, supplies, parts, equipment?
- What are the limits to their authority?

Until those and other similar questions about the job itself are answered, you can't determine whether or not a given candidate has the skills, attitude, or knowledge to do it well.

Forcing yourself to take this step also helps you avoid the single biggest mistake shop owners make when choosing a manager: promoting or hiring someone just because they are good in their current job. Someone with a magician's touch with the spray gun doesn't necessarily have the communication skills to handle recalcitrant employees. Even a great upholsterer doesn't need to know how to motivate people. A good shop supervisor needs technical skills, but they need managerial skills—or at least instincts—even more.

If you're promoting from within, there's also the danger of negatively impacting your shop's productivity by taking your best technician off the line and putting them in the office, so you'll want to be sure that you're producing a net gain before you make the move. The potential for a double whammy exists, too, since the great technician may turn out to be a terrible manager who reduces the staff's effectiveness by under- or over-managing, mis-directing, or even de-motivating them.

Thou art manager

Few business owners would hire a kid off the street and turn him loose to cut sunroof holes in customers' cars the first day, but that's generally the way most companies start their managers. They promote the person, maybe have a team meeting to tell everybody about it, and then tap them on the shoulder with some words of wisdom that amount to, "Now thou art a manager. Go forth thou and manage." No training, no easing into the job, no transition period. It's sink or swim. Manage or fail.

Maybe that's an exaggeration, but not by much. No one expects you to send your new supervisor to Harvard Business School, but a little time invested in equipping them with the managerial skills they need will pay off in the long run. At the least, they need to learn that a good manager doesn't just issue orders; he listens, too. He doesn't always have to give an immediate answer to every question; it's better to look it up and be right. A good manager criticizes in private but praises in public. He concentrates on his employees' performance, not their personalities. The lessons a new manager needs to learn are many, so it makes sense to give them some time—and direction—to learn them.

In many ways, it's easier to hire a supervisor from outside than it is to promote someone from the ranks. The supervisor you bring in probably doesn't have prior relationships with the staff and all the baggage attached to them. His or her opinions will carry at least some additional weight simply because he's an outsider who, the staff should assume, has wider experience than they do. Not having worked side by side with them, they also won't have (yet) seen any weaknesses. The outsider will still have to prove themselves, but they'll start from a different place than the person you promote from within.

There's a lot to be said for moving someone up from the ranks, though, too. They know your operation already, have relationships with customers, and one with you, too, which makes communication easier and more productive. Hopefully, a level of trust with the other employees will also exist, which is something an outsider will need time to develop. Besides, promoting from within almost always does great things for morale.

Managing the manager

Baggage handling—redefining the relationship with people he or she previously worked side-by-side with—is something you and the newly-promoted manager need to deal with right away. It's not as big a problem as you might think, but it can lead to other problems down the line unless everyone realizes that things are different now. Socialization is going to change, for example. Good Ol' Joe can still get together with the guys for a couple of beers after hours, but he's going to have to watch the opinions he expresses a little more carefully. He's also going to have to be careful not to show any favoritism when it comes to assignments.

Another factor that bears examination is your relationship with the new supervisor. Whether it's a new position in your shop or a new person in the job, it's a good idea to keep some things in mind. A big one is the relationship between authority and responsibility. Does your manager have responsibility for results? If so, how do you measure them? By the amount of work that gets done, the profitability of the jobs as a whole or individually, the satisfaction expressed by your customers? There are many ways to define success, but only those that are specific can be measured. And you can only hold someone responsible for results if those results can be measured.

You also can't expect someone to take responsibility for something without giving them the authority to get it done. Authority means the ability to make a decision and have it hold up. Second-guessing is the quickest way to destroy a manager's self-confidence and undermine their relationship with the people who work for them. If you take away the manager's authority—either intentionally or by accident—you've effectively demoted them.

But managers need managing, too. They respond to praise, especially when it's given in front of the rest of the staff, and they need critical appraisals from time to time—but always delivered in private.

Hiring a good manager can do a lot for you and your business. A manager can give the company owner time during the day to step back and see the bigger picture. He can help spot problems

150

and deal with them in the formative stages. He can allow you to expand without losing control over the quality of your company's work. If these are things you want to accomplish, it may be time to hire a manager.

Chapter 27

Managing Einstein

"Within the next year, I'm going to choose one of you to take my place."

Three sales reps sat facing me across my desk. I had used the phrase "bright, conscientious, and aggressive" to describe each one in their last performance review. Privately, I also gave each one five stars for creativity, a trait not often considered important for sales people but one I personally feel is essential to high achievement. The creative salesperson found ways to produce orders. My choice was going to be difficult but I felt confident that any one of them could do the job.

The three may have possessed some common talents, but they couldn't have been more different in background, ambitions, and personality.

Don came from the upscale New York suburb of Scarsdale. His father owned a very successful medical publishing business that he had started with a quarterly newsletter for pediatricians and built into a thirty-title house with over four hundred employees. Don worked for his father briefly after college but entered our training program to prove he could make it on his own. The fact that he was unobtrusively gay both complicated his relationship with his father and fueled his desire to publicly succeed.

Stephen's family had money once, too, but lost most of it when an over-leveraged Manhattan real estate venture failed. He lived on the upper East Side with an older brother who was using family connections to hustle a Wall Street career. Stephen saw our industry, television advertising, as the perfect milieu for the hip, fast-living life he wanted to live. He dressed sharp, ate in the trendiest restaurants, and had a cell phone permanently attached to his ear. Stephen also made smooth, well-polished presentations and let nothing stop him from reaching the decision maker.

Gerry lived in a row house in Queens with his stereotypical Irish Catholic parents and five brothers and sisters. If his mother had been less diligent in pushing her children to better themselves, he could easily have ended up working on the docks instead of Madison Avenue. Gerry had a great head for numbers, an earthy wit, and a determination that could crack the hardest buyer's facade. He approached his career as a series of fist fights, and took deep pride in winning every one.

After I explained that I would be moving up in the company and that I would choose my successor based on sales performance and initiative, they left my office quietly, each lost in his own thoughts. Determination to win glowed in their eyes.

Sales in the next few months were spectacular. I congratulated myself on a brilliant strategy and started looking forward to my next job. One of the funny things about managing bright, creative people, though, is that you never really know what they're going to do next. They're inquisitive—they want to know what really happens when you place one more straw on the camel's back. They're inventive—if one solution doesn't work, they make up another one. They're confident—failure happens but mostly to lesser beings.

One afternoon, Stephen walked into my office unusually rattled. I knew he had been pitching a baseball sponsorship to his largest ad agency client that day. It had obviously not gone well.

"You're probably going to get a phone call from Susan Myers," he said. "She's pretty mad and said she wants me off the agency." He couldn't look me in the eye so he straightened the crease in his trousers and inspected the shine on his shoes.

"What happened?"

"I pitched the sponsorship to Gary Maloney and he said he liked it but Susan would have to sign off on it. So I went to Susan's office and her secretary told me she was in the conference room. I could see a few people in there with her, but they didn't seem to be doing much. So I just opened the door and asked Susan if I could see her for a few minutes."

I was incredulous. "You walked into a meeting?!"

"Well, everybody in the agency seems to really like me and I thought Susan wouldn't mind since it was me. Besides, I wanted to sell the deal before the spots are sold out."

"So you thought the rules of common courtesy don't apply to you?"

"Sure they do. But I figured I could talk my way out of it."

As his manager, I was faced with a dilemma. Stephen hadn't exactly murdered anybody and he had followed one of the prime rules of sales—get to the decision maker. On the other hand, he had risked our lucrative relationship with that decision maker by stepping over a boundary. I admired his determination but deplored his judgment. He found a solution to the problem but didn't fully think through all the consequences of that solution. It's a common flaw in the creative mindset. Smoothing over the situation with Susan Myers was easy for me. The harder task was figuring out how to keep Stephen on a short leash without damaging his enthusiasm?

Soon after, Gerry presented another difficult situation. This one sprang from overconfidence and thinking too fast on his feet. He brought it into my office one afternoon.

"I screwed up," he started.

"What's going on?" I replied.

"Do you remember the order I brought in for the Central Pennsylvania Fair?"

"Sure. It was more than we expected to get."

"Well, I didn't mean to, but I told a lie to the buyer. That's why we got such a large share of the budget."

"That's not good. What happened?"

"We were talking about unmeasured audiences. You know, like military barracks and vacation homes that watch TV but aren't counted by the rating services? I remembered that Central Pennsylvania has a big Amish population and I assumed they wouldn't be measured because of their isolation or something. But, since they would be logical customers for the Fair, I told the buyer that we would be delivering them as a bonus audience. She agreed to give me a bigger share but I have to get back to her with an estimate on the size of the Amish audience."

"That's going to be hard to do, isn't it?"

"Yeah. I know," he said. "The Amish don't have electricity—they can't watch TV. I found that out after I turned the order in and started doing the research. Now what do I do?"

The answer for Gerry was obvious; tell the buyer about his mistake and take the consequences. The answer for me, though, wasn't so clear. I don't believe he intentionally lied but his know-it-all attitude made it look like he did. He was so excited about discovering a new way to sell the package that he didn't check his facts first. His imagination led him beyond the edge. How could I make him self-regulate his ideas without smothering his imaginative approach to the business?

Don's creativity got us into another kind of hot water. This time it was all about an unpaid bill for sixty dollars that nearly cost us several million.

One morning I received a letter from Sally Thompson, buying supervisor at one of our largest agency customers, BBD&O. They bought time from us all over the country for big-spending clients like Pepsi and Dodge. Sally's letter started out like this:

"Dear Dave:

Please be advised that you will not receive any orders for any of our clients during the next quarter due to the recent actions of your rep, Don Mariso."

I read through the letter and the enclosures before I called Don in to tell me his side of the story. When he sat down, I handed the pages to him without comment. He turned very pale.

"I guess I made a major mess, didn't I?"

"That's putting it mildly," I said. "Now tell me how this happened."

He took a deep breath before he started.

"We had an order for Pillsbury to run in June in the late news on our station in Burlington. There was a breaking news story that caused an overrun one night and the spot ran later than usual. BBD&O refused to pay for the spot so accounting turned it over to me to straighten out."

This was a routine situation and was part of the normal give and take that occurs in a fluid business like television advertising. I asked him why it got out of hand.

"They had no right to do that—the spot ran in the program they ordered. So I took it back to the buyer and demanded payment. She didn't want to mess with the paperwork for something that small and told me to get lost. So I went to her supervisor and got the same treatment. In the meantime, accounting is calling me every other day asking where the check is.

"I didn't know what else to do, so I wrote this letter to Joseph Frazier, the CEO of Pillsbury. I thought it would be a way to break through their indifference."

One of Sally's enclosures was a copy of the letter Don wrote. It basically told Frazier that his advertising agency was giving his company a black eye by refusing to pay the overdue bill. It also asked for the sixty dollars. Sally had also sent me the letter she received from Frazier, who wanted to know who this Don guy was and why he was demanding sixty dollars from the Pillsbury corporation. Don had committed a major sin by interfering in the relationship between the agency and its client. He was legally correct, but had killed a flea with a hand grenade.

"I have to take you off the agency, Don," I said. "I also want you to write a full apology to Sally and Joseph Frazier. I'll send it with the letter I'm going to write to them."

That was the easy part of my decision. The harder one was finding a way to make Ron realize that he must involve other people—his manager, for instance—in his work. He was part of a team whether he wanted to be or not. Many creative people are stubbornly individualistic. They're not afraid to go it alone. In fact, they often believe they produce the best results when they fly solo. That approach works great when they paint a picture; it fails horribly when they try to build a mile-long suspension bridge.

Creative people have many double-edged traits that make managing them interesting, to put it mildly. Imagine supervising the work of a person who's probably smarter than you (and knows it), has limitless curiosity about everything from your company's products to the inner workings of the international space station, and won't quit working on a problem until it's solved—even if you tell him to. In other words, what would it be like to manage Einstein?

- Creative people ask "why." This isn't because they are disputatious but rather because knowing the reasons behind a decision or the history of a policy helps them look for ways to use or improve it. Janese Swanson, founder of GirlTech, says she spent many childhood hours taking things apart just to see how they worked. Knowing how something works marks the first step toward maximizing its utility. Knowing why a goal exists frees the innovator to look for alternative ways to achieve it.

- Creative people are discontent. They don't whine, but they are never fully satisfied with the status quo. The urge to change energizes their work. It also pushes them to strive for perfection. Bob Moses, a math teacher in Cambridge, Massachusetts, was one of the chief organizers of the Freedom Summer of 1964, when hundreds of college students from around the country went to Mississippi to protest racial inequality. He has devoted his life to causing change. Moses' dedication continued as he flew from Cambridge every week to Jackson, MS, to teach algebra at all-black Lanier High School.

- Creative people look for challenges. They constantly test themselves, often against standards that only they recognize. That's how they improve themselves. Once a task or skill is mastered, they often lose interest in it and start looking for another test. Venture capitalist Ann Winblad worked for the Federal Reserve Bank in Minneapolis, started a software company, Open Systems, went to work as a consultant for Microsoft, Apple and IBM, wrote a book on object-oriented programming, and co-founded Hummer Winblad Venture Partners, a $95 million venture capital fund. To some, her resume would indicate a lack of direction. To a manager acquainted with innovators, though, it would show a constant quest for different challenges.

• Creative people seek knowledge for its own sake. This inquisitiveness leads them often into seemingly non-productive areas. Oceanographer Dr. Sylvia Earle, former chief scientist of the National Oceanographic and Atmospheric Administration, likes to read the encyclopedia, a habit she acquired as an inquisitive child. A stockbroker studying the thoughts of Marcus Aurelius may appear to be engaged in highbrow time-killing. Recalling those ideas in times of stress, though, can be very helpful.

• Creative people persevere in the face of failure. Most sales people give up when a prospect refuses to return their calls for an appointment. It's easier to move on to a new one after three or four tries. The creative salesperson, on the other hand, doesn't stop. If phone calls don't work, they send a fax. If the fax doesn't work, they send flowers. If the flowers don't work, they send a singing telegram delivered by a gorilla. Bioethicist Dr. Arthur Caplan points out, "For every idea that has worked that makes it into a medical publication or headline, there are a hundred that aren't because they didn't work."

• Creative people live comfortably in their imagination. Weird ideas don't threaten them, they entertain them. As you would expect, they love brainstorming meetings. A creative person can also brainstorm by themselves, looking for the kernel of a practical idea hidden in a wild, outrageous scenario that only they can see. As a child in the Bronx, jazz musician Don Byron, was kept indoors much of the time by a near crippling asthma. But isolation didn't confine him. "A lot of the [music] that I've investigated in my life," Byron says, he first encountered "within the walls of my

bedroom in my parents' house." He found it within his own imagination.

- Creative people are optimists. Any problem can be solved.
The sure way to fail is to not try. Failure just marks another step on
the road to the solution. Successful New York real estate manager
Richmond McCoy founded UrbanAmerica, the first real estate investment company to focus on distressed urban areas, a market
sinfully ignored by most moneymen. Where others saw high risk
and low returns, McCoy saw opportunity.

- Creative people make mistakes. In fact, they usually make
lots of them because they try so many different ideas so many
times with no assurance that they will work. Our society tends to
look on failure as a mark of inadequacy or ineptness. The creative
person, though, sees a mistake as just another part of the learning
process. It took medical professor Graeme Clark and a multidisci-
plinary team based at the University of Melbourne 18 years to turn
a theory of his into a commercial reality. The cochlear implant, or
"bionic ear," he invented has allowed even profoundly deaf people
to "hear."

- Creative people take risks and love rewards. With no fear
of failure and a certainty of success, the creative person doesn't
hesitate to explore uncharted territory, use untried techniques, or
tackle previously unsolvable problems. The rewards craved can
take many forms; recognition, money, advancement, even the as-
signment of new and bigger challenges. The satisfaction of a job
well done doesn't last long unless it's attached to another reward.
It's notable how many innovative superstars monetized their talents

at an early age. Ray Kurzweil, for example, started a business matching high school students with colleges through a computer program he wrote during his second year at the Massachusetts Institute of Technology. After this early financial success, he went on to develop the first flatbed scanner, the first text-to-speech synthesizer, and the first program that allows computers to recognize text printed in any style of type.

- Creative people are supremely confident. Put another way, they often have huge egos. Most people, if they even think about it at all, don't consider themselves creative. This sets the creative person apart from the majority. Society also generally applauds its creative members for their outsized contributions to improving the quality of life. So the creative person has the opportunity to step onto a pedestal. National Medal of Science winner Carl Djerassi, the father of the oral contraceptive, says that a creative person is obsessed by wanting to read his own obituary.

Each of these traits cuts both ways. They can lead to big success or huge failure. The manager simply leads the creative person toward one and away from the other. Then they all live happily ever after, just like in all the other fairy tales.

We don't live or operate in a fairy tale world, though. We live in the world of Don, Stephen, and Gerry, creative people whose mistakes could have been costly to the organization and hard on other people. As their manager, I had to cope with those mistakes while maintaining the momentum of their successes—because that's profitable for the organization and allowed us to produce results we wouldn't have without them.

Creative people drive most successful organizations. They are literally the most important assets of many companies like advertising agencies, movie studios, and publishers. Their research also fires the growth of the leading technology, pharmaceutical, and communications companies. Less obvious, though, are the creative people that design new financial instruments for Wall Street or the creative marketers who fill planes and hotel rooms in the travel industry. Look inside a growth company and you will find creative people in nearly every office.

Then look into the corner offices and you will find the managers who lead these creative people. They don't have a manual to teach them how to manage their unique staffs. One doesn't exist. They've learned their leadership skills on the job, dealing with the quandaries, dilemmas, and wonderful opportunities they face every day.

Like the ones generated by Ron, Stephen, and Mike. Should one of them be promoted?

I based my decision on many factors, weighing the problems each had created along with their temperaments, personalities, communication skills, business knowledge and the many other subjective criteria by which managers are chosen.

Stephen's faux-pas led me to conclude that he might be inclined to let his personal ambitions outweigh his concern for the feelings of other people. Don's showed me that he probably wouldn't become a good team player, much less a good team leader. The nod went to Gerry because his mistake was a simple matter of over-eagerness blinding him to a blank spot in his knowledge.

Since his error didn't stem from a flaw in his ability to deal with other people, I felt comfortable promoting him.

Chapter 28
Case Study: The Employee Family
"Teamwork and mutual respect are part of everyday life at Charles River Apparel"

When Barry Lipsett bought Charles River Apparel from his father, Walter, in 1993, the Medford, MA., outerwear company was losing money on annual sales of $3 million. Now, revenues are comfortably north of $30 million, and profits aren't a problem, even though Charles River competes with behemoths like Reebok (a subsidiary of Adidas AG) and Nike.

How has Barry done it? The secret, he says, is to treat everyone like family members and let the profits take care of themselves.

"My goal isn't just making a dollar," says Barry, 47. "Because we have done well, we've been able to give back and do the things I'd like to do. I hope that attitude contributes to the company's profitability, but that's not the reason we do it."

Along the way, Charles River has picked up a boatload of honors. It has been listed in Boston magazine as one of the area's "Best Places to Work." In 2005, it received the Family Business of the Year award from the Advertising Specialty Institute, a promotional-products association. For several years, it's been named as one of the Top 100 Sporting Goods Manufacturers in the U.S. by

Sporting Edge Magazine, the publication of the Sporting Goods Manufacturers Association.

Many of Charles River's approximately 10,000 customers are advertising specialty or promotional product distributors, who then apply their customers' message to the garment for use as sales incentives, in marketing campaigns or at corporate events and celebrations. The 12,000 employees at Hackensack Medical Center in New Jersey, for example, received Charles River-made jackets at Christmas two years in a row. Charles River has provided apparel for customers licensed to sell gear commemorating the Super Bowl, World Series, NCAA basketball tournament and golf's Ryder Cup.

The company's second-largest market consists of athletic teams, mostly sold through sporting goods stores and other distributors who apply team logos, names, and numbers to uniforms for local high school and other amateur teams. Next are college bookstores. Charles River is licensed to create merchandise for hundreds of schools, including Harvard, MIT, Yale and the universities of Michigan and Wisconsin. The company also supplies Barnes and Noble, which leases about 500 college bookstores.

Then there is the resort market, especially in the Northeast. "If you go to Cape Cod, Martha's Vineyard, or some of the other resort areas around the country," Barry says, "you'll find a lot of Charles River rainwear, although it may carry the local store's logo." The company also sells to retailers like Nordstrom, L.L. Bean, Bloomingdale's, and Talbots.

Though Barry sees opportunities for further growth, he says he's hesitant to make any moves that would jeopardize Charles

River's reputation. "Our strategy for the last 15 years has been manageable growth," Barry says. "We try to run the business without getting ahead of ourselves. If you grow 30%, we can't offer the service we like. In November, 2006, we did grow 30%, and that kind of hurt our service."

Birth of a business

Walter Lipsett founded Charles River Apparel in 1983 because he was bored. The steel company he had started in 1948 with his father, Central Steel Supply, was "Providing a nice living," he says, and he needed a new challenge, so he plunged into a rainwear business named in honor of his rowing days at the Massachusetts Maritime Academy. The original concept was to sell raincoats to retailers, but it never really took off.

Barry—who had joined Charles River in 1987 after a stint in sales at the steel company, preceded by college at the University of Wisconsin in Madison and a short career at the Chicago Mercantile Exchange—tried to push the Charles River brand in several markets. But the real turning point came in 1990 when, flying home from a Florida vacation, Walter read an article in the in-flight magazine about the advertising specialty business. "I thought that would be a wonderful market for our product," he recalls.

He and Barry investigated the field at a New England Promotional Products Association trade show. "We both knew that was the market for Charles River Apparel," Walter says.

Today Charles River has about 80 full-time staffers, a far cry from Walter's five original employees who sold rain jackets and trench coats to department stores. Barry is now the sole owner of the company, and several family members help out. His sister Julie Lipsett, is the human resources director; his wife, Deborah, works in customer service. Until her untimely death from cancer in 2006, another sister, Susan de Vries, worked in sales.

Walter is still very active in the company, too, although on a part-time basis. "My dad and I share an office," Barry says. "We have a sign on the door with his name that says 'Mentor.'" The two talk by phone several times a day and lunch together frequently when Walter is not wintering in Florida, where he spends four months a year.

Barry says he was able to find and exploit the various markets where Charles River competes because he hired his own sales force instead of relying on manufacturers' reps who handle multiple lines. Charles River's sales staff includes a friend of Barry's from middle school, a cousin and a rep who's been with the company since it started. "They may not all be family members, but they're like family members," Barry says, then adds with a chuckle, "They feel like they can yell at me when things go wrong."

Over the years, Barry has supported a long list of local and national charitable organizations and has received regional awards in recognition of his efforts. Non-profits he's involved with include Toys for Tots, the American Cancer Society and the Special Olympics.

When Hurricane Katrina struck the Gulf Coast, "We got our customers and employees involved," Barry relates. "Our employees filled a minivan with donations of merchandise we had, then drove it to Louisiana, stopping at customers along the way to collect contributions from them." Barry drove the van to New Jersey, then passed the wheel to a succession of Charles River reps and customers to complete the trip to New Orleans. The Charles River apparel items donated were worth $35,000. The van also carried merchandise donated by W.B. Mason, a Massachusetts office supplies company, for schools and students.

That wasn't the end of the journey: the company donated the van itself to School Times in Baton Rouge, La., a distributor of Charles River Apparel that was affected by Katrina. That company used the vehicle to shuttle hurricane victims to and from shelters. Afterward, Charles River donated more merchandise to school athletic programs in areas stricken by Katrina.

This kind of collaboration among Charles River owners, employees and customers doesn't just happen in times of national disaster, say those involved in the company. Teamwork and mutual respect are part of everyday life at Charles River Apparel, they report.

'A very caring group'

Charles River Apparel provides a host of perks and benefits to its employees, from commonplace offerings like a matching 401(k) plan, tuition reimbursement and discounts on merchandise to less standard privileges like van pools and free meals. The company's health care plan covers medical, dental and vision expenses; infertility treatments; and chiropractic, acupuncture and homeopathic therapies. Benefits are offered to same- and opposite-sex domestic partners. At the end of 2006, Charles River spent $6,500 on new equipment for the 2,000-square-foot company fitness center, complete with shower, changing room and TV.

Barry gives bonuses to all employees, not just the managers. The size of the bonus is discretionary. He says year-end bonuses for an order picker could be $500 to $800. Customer-service personnel, especially those who have been with the company for 15 or 20 years, get as much as $3,000. And everybody in the company receives a $25 gift certificate from a local grocery store at Thanksgiving.

"If we have a real good year, which we've had the last few years, we add a profit-sharing bonus, too," Barry says. That bonus usually goes to managers, although it's sometimes distributed to the rank and file.

Such generous benefits can both hurt and help a company, according to Paul Rich, Principal in the Business Consulting Group of Rothstein Kass in New York. "For a company to be competitive," he says, "they want to be the employer of choice, which means higher benefits. If they're in an industry where margins are low, though, they could be so social-minded it makes them non-competitive. On the other hand, you can also have companies that become less competitive because of high turnover and low efficiency due to not being generous enough."

Barry says he and Walter always looked on liberal employee benefits as just another way to reinvest profits in the company. He pays for them, in part, by limiting his own compensation. In addition to his salary, which was smaller than some of the company's sales reps, he says, Barry took a dividend equal to only five percent of the company's profits last year. "There have been many companies in the apparel industry who grew really fast, but the owners took all the profits out and didn't reinvest in the company. When fashions changed and times got tough, they didn't have a company left."

Individual employees are treated as, well, individuals. On Sept. 11, 2001, sales rep Gary Schwartz had been with Charles River less than three years, but his sales were skyrocketing—up 40% for the year up to that dreadful day. After the terrorists attacked, his phones were dead. His customers couldn't call from Long Island and parts of New York because of the loss of the Verizon facility at ground zero. For someone whose income is commission-generated, this situation could have been devastating. "We paid him the same amount of commission he made the year before for the last four months, even though his sales were down substantially," Barry says.

Accounting and licensing manager Sharon Hennessy has worked at Charles River Apparel since 1984; her sister works at Central Steel. "From Barry right on down, it's a very caring group and always has been," Hennessy says. One year, the company sent her and her husband to the Bahamas. "It was just a thank-you for what I've done over the years," Hennessy says. "It wasn't a bonus, an anniversary or any other special occasion--it was a pure 'thank you.'"

Hennessy also praises "the little things Barry does" like the "pre-crunch lunch" in September before busy season starts, complete with Nestlé Crunch bars for everyone; the sundaes on hot summer days. "Those are the kinds of things that they do that you won't find anyplace else," Hennessy says.

Beyond 'schmoozing'

The Lipsetts stress their devotion to over-the-top customer service as a worthwhile end in itself. Walter built the steel company on a policy of turning orders around within a day if he possibly could, one of the few ways he could stand out in a commodity industry like steel. "The order was not the key issue," Walter says. "It was providing the proper service—or telling the customer that I couldn't. I was always truthful. Under-promise, over-perform, that's the key."

Today, Charles River has the same goal, a valuable edge when its customer's customer may be depending on the arrival of 500 jackets in time for a big, expensive Super Bowl party. The company does what has to be done to make sure it happens.

"Some companies, if you call at four o'clock, you'll be told the shipping department is closed and you'll have to wait for tomorrow," says Lisa McCullagh, owner of corporate gift company Scarborough & Tweed in Pleasantville, NY. "If you call Charles River at six o'clock and explain your emergency, they will put the order in their car and drive it to the UPS terminal." Service like that doesn't just happen, McCullagh says; it must be built into the company culture. "I think that comes from having a family-style company where everybody there cares about the bottom line," she says.

John Medlin, owner of Rockland Athletic Supplies in Rockland, MA., has been a Charles River customer since he opened his own family business in 1984. He confirms Charles River's deep devotion to customer service. "If I need something they don't have in stock, my Charles River rep will e-mail around to his other customers to see if they have any," he says. "They'll even go to other orders that might be waiting to be shipped for some other reason and see if what I need is in them and they can ship it to me without causing the other customer a problem." Medlin adds without hesitation, "They bend over backwards for us, and they always have."

Charles River involves its customers in product decisions. "As we develop our lines," Barry relates, "we talk to our customers about it. For example, our designer just e-mailed the design for a pair of warm-up pants to about 20 accounts to get feedback on it. The reps are part of that process, too. It's very collaborative."

"If I need something specific or have a question," McCullagh says, "I can call Barry and he will be very attentive and answer it, which is amazing considering the size of his company." Barry might not be able to personally answer questions from all 10,000 of the company's customers, but you get the impression he'd like to try.

Barry says he inherited his propensity to "schmooze" customers from his father, who developed this talent in the steel industry. "He is really good at helping the reps bring in business," Barry says of Walter. "He loves finding them new leads and helping them with accounts they can't sell. He loves telling stories." Charles River frequently sends flowers and other tokens of appreciation to mark births, deaths, graduations, anniversaries and other occasions in the lives of its customers. The family and the company reps also socialize with customers a lot, bringing them to Boston for sporting events, parties and picnics.

"We have a personal relationship with them," Medlin says. "The first catalog I give to my customers is Charles River's."

Partnering with suppliers

Like nearly all U.S. apparel companies, Charles River designs its own products but has them manufactured overseas. The company currently works with factories in Pakistan, Taiwan, China, the Philippines, Vietnam and Cambodia. Walter says he's always believed that "If you have the right relationship, it's like a partnership. Then the supplier knows that their best interests are our best interests." He tells the story of the supplier in Pakistan who got into some cash flow difficulty not long after Barry took over the company. Charles River helped him out by purchasing the fabrics and trim for him and having it shipped to his factory for assembly. "He never forgot that," Walter says. "Now, we don't even need to inspect his goods when they come in; we know they're going to be perfect."

The company doesn't have much choice when it comes to manufacturing overseas, according to Barry. "The type of apparel we sell hasn't been made in America for decades," he explains. He also recognizes the sometimes difficult conditions under which his overseas vendors operate. "I know the families that operate the factories," he says. "I've been to their houses; they've been to mine. I know some of the kids. It's a relationship that's similar to the one we have with our customers and our employees." That relationship extends to the supplier's employees, too. In one instance, Charles

River built a well so the workers could have clean water at a factory in the Philippines. "We upgraded their kitchen facility, too," Barry says. "It's not always as easy as we'd like, but we try." In addition to personal visits by Charles River's managers, they retain an inspection agency to insure that no child labor is used and that workers are treated humanely.

Building bridges like that helps Charles River meet its corporate goals, too. "When we purchase, it's based on a forecast," Barry explains. "Ninety-five percent of our orders need to be shipped within 24 hours. It takes four or five months to get products from overseas, so we forecast extra inventory by style, color and size. If we run low on an item and our supplier can speed up their delivery, it's a huge value that they add." The mills that make the cloth and the factories that stitch together the garments are usually separate companies, often located in different countries, so Charles River's suppliers must keep fabric and accessories inventory on hand to meet the need for a quick response. This requires an act of faith on the suppliers' part—another benefit of a close relationship with Charles River Apparel.

For Barry Lipsett and his family, the focus on people and partnerships has paid off handsomely. As Walter says, "If you do things right, the future will take care of itself."

Originally published in Family Business, www.familybusinessmagazine.com.

Section Four

Sales & Marketing

Good customers are hard to find, but they are easy to lose. Keeping your current customers happy may be the most important marketing strategy for any small business owner. From small things like your telephone greeting to large ones like how you handle complaints, everything you and your staff does affects your customer relationships. That's why the Dynamic Manager Guides include two other volumes devoted to the subjects, *The Dynamic Manager's Guide To Marketing & Advertising* and *The Dynamic Manager's Guide To Creative Selling*. The chapters in this section cover new topics in this nearly endless field.

Small business marketing should be an active process—especially when the economy is in the doldrums. Salespeople in stores don't have to wait for the customer to buy something—they can increase sales and earn bigger commissions with some simple creative selling techniques. The company owner or manager can sell more by using creative marketing methods to present product benefits, overcome objections, and close the sale. When times are tough and the competition is cutting back, the successful manager takes advantage of the opportunity to build market share.

On another front, whether you're an exhibitor or a visitor, trade shows can help build your business. You can meet new customers and suppliers, scope out the competition, catch up on industry trends and gossip, and even make a splash in the media. But there's more to it than buying an ticket to the expo. This handbook will show you how to maximize the return on your trade show dollar.

Chapter 29

Creative Marketing For Tough Times

"Block out all the negative headlines."

There are three kinds of small business owners: Takers, Getters, and Go-Getters.

"Takers" go to work in the morning and take whatever business comes in during the rest of the day. "Getters" open their store and then stand outside to get any business that walks by. "Go-Getters" don't wait for their store to open; they go get business wherever they can find it. Guess which one does best when the economy softens?

The Go Getter, of course, sells more in any economy. When times are tough, though, they really outperform. If you're not a Go Getter already, would you like to learn how?

Becoming a Go Getter

The first step is the hardest: fight your instincts to cut your marketing budget. Any good business person knows you should cut expenses during times of falling revenues. Unfortunately, our inclination is to make the easiest cuts first. Because marketing expenses like advertising, promotions, and outside sales aren't ongoing like the rent, insurance, and payroll, they are easy to slash. The easy way, though, is seldom the best way.

Bad things happen when you stop going after business. Prospective customers never learn about you. Current customers forget about you. During tough times there may be fewer customers of either kind, but there are some—and some is better than none when it comes to sales. This principle, by the way, doesn't apply just to your business but to your corporate customers' businesses as well. Since most of them use gift baskets as marketing tools, it's a good idea to point out during your sales pitch that cutting back on such a valuable customer-relationship tool generates false savings.

Good things happen when you continue—or even increase—your marketing during tough times. Consider the findings of a survey done in 2001 by Yankelovich Partners/Harris Interactive, Inc., for the trade association, American Business Media. They found that 86% of the 505 executives surveyed said that when they see advertising by a company in a down economy, it keeps that company top-of-mind when they make purchasing decisions, and it makes them feel more positive about that company's commitment to its products and services.

Seize the opportunity

What's more, your marketing can even be more effective when times are tough for the simple reason that your competitors may well be cutting back. Think of a crowded room where everyone is talking at once. Any individual voice is hard to distinguish, isn't it? If one person keeps talking after everybody else shuts up, though, you hear that voice loud and clear. Once again, a good point to make to your corporate customers.

Perhaps the best reason to keep going after more business during a downturn is what that strategy does to your business when the economy heats up again. Imagine two bicyclists pedaling along a level road. Equal effort by each one keeps them side-by-side. But what if they start up a hill and the going gets harder? If they both get off to walk their bikes to the top, they'll reach it at the same time. If one keeps pedaling, though, that person will get to the top first. Tired, maybe, but in the lead. And that lead will increase as they travel over the next level stretch because their competitor is still back there pushing their bike up the hill. Marketing is more than just an impetus to sales today; it's an investment in sales in the future.

One of the most significant historical recessions was 1980-82. McGraw-Hill Research analyzed the sales of 600 companies not just during the recession but for three years after. They found that firms that maintained or increased their advertising expenditures during the 1980-82 recession achieved higher sales growth both during the downturn and for three years after it ended! By 1985, sales of companies that were aggressive recession advertisers had risen 256% over those that didn't keep up their spending.

Go Getter tactics

Retail Go-Getters should maintain their consumer advertising exposure—although not necessarily their spending. Most advertising media suffer pretty badly during downturns, so they're usually willing to negotiate with a sharper pencil. That means you may be able to get the same amount of ad space, time, or services for fewer dollars. If you want to really create a stir, keep your spending up—

you should be able to increase your exposure at no extra cost by taking advantage of the soft advertising market conditions.

Your advertising message (retail or corporate) should center on value. Not price—value. Value is the relationship between what the customer pays and the benefits they receive. If you can convince the customer that they're going to strengthen a friendship, enjoy a better love life, or increase their sales by buying a product or service from you, your price will look better every time. The inverse is also true, by the way; if they don't believe they will receive these or other benefits, it doesn't matter how little you charge.

Go-Getters who concentrate on corporate sales step up their marketing efforts during tough times. They make more calls on current customers to encourage them to keep buying. They do more prospecting for new customers, too, whether it be through advertising, direct sales, or both. And they explore more markets. Maybe, for example, you've avoided a given market niche in the past because it's small and the price point is low; now may be the time to give that decision a second look.

Stay positive

You've no doubt noticed that all of this means more work, too. Of course it does! Pedaling that bicycle uphill requires more effort. That's why taking the first step, committing to an aggressive marketing strategy, is so important.

There's also no question that you have to be an optimist to be a Go Getter. You have to block out all the negative headlines and ignore all the "woe is me" talk from everyone around you. If a headline starts pushing you into a funk, remember that there are at least two sides to every news story. If you read, for example, that unemployment is nine percent, remind yourself that ninety-one percent of the workforce is still drawing a paycheck!

And the next time a customer or employee starts pleading poverty, remember that they probably drove their ten-mile-per-gallon SUV to buy a $3.95 low-fat double-shot latte (otherwise known as a cup of coffee) on their way to work this morning. How tough can times be?

Chapter 30

Case Study: Multiply Your Profits
"Multiple locations and business extensions
build specialty retail profits."

Looking for a challenge? Try operating a second, third, or even fourth retail location. You might think multiple locations simply means multiple headaches, but that's not necessarily so. They can also mean multiple profits.

That's been the experience of Diane and Madis Sulg, who own two Maddi's Gallery locations. They opened their original art and craft gallery in Charlotte, NC, in 2002, and the second, in suburban Birkedale Village, two years later. "It just made sense for us," she says. "It allowed us to vary our inventory, share the talents of our management, and expand our customer base." The couple's daughter and son-in-law, Michaella and Jon Dalton, manage the new gallery.

The single most important factor in the success of a second store is the same as the first—location, according to the Sulgs. Birkedale Village is a planned development with shopping areas, apartments and condos near tony Lake Norman. Madis describes it as "a mall-like location with nice upscale shops." This contrasts with their smaller (1500-square-feet) original gallery, which is in a neighborhood shopping area. The two locations are about 20 miles apart.

They didn't choose Birkedale Village at random. The original gallery attracted customers from the vicinity, but they often complained about how difficult it was to make the trip. "There was a high demographic in that area," Diane explains. "What used to be small summer cottages have turned into multi-million dollar mansions. We felt there was opportunity there."

The two locations have developed markedly different clientele, a theme which other gallery owners who operate multiple locations repeat consistently. "The market for the original store is a little more traditional," according to Diane, "while we sell things in the other store that are a little more contemporary." Both stores carry Michelle Allen-designed clocks, for example, but the Birkedale Village gallery sold more clocks in one year than the Charlotte shop sold in four. "We joked that no one in Lake Norman knew what time it was before we got there," she says.

What about even more locations? Sandy Sardella, owner of Pismo Fine Glass in Denver, Beaver Creek, Aspen, and Vail, Colorado, says the biggest different between running two locations and four is "You are twice as tired!" Even though there are many advantages to multiple locations, she says, "Each location has its own personality and clientele. You need to be aware of the personalities of your staff at each location and of the personalities of your customers. Even between galleries you have different customer bases."

Different marketing

It's a good idea to try out different marketing ideas for the same lines in different stores because operating multiple art and craft galleries isn't the same as replicating hamburger stands or coffee shops across the nation. In the Maddi's mall location, for example, they place a table with jewelry marked "$25 and under" near the front entrance to tempt the casual walk-by shopper. The original store carries the same line, but displays it traditionally.

Diane Campbell, opened Yikes! Gallery in Center Harbor, NH, with her husband Kevin in 1992. Ten years later, they opened a second shop in Laconia, NH, and discovered they were serving two different markets. "We took the best sellers from Center Harbor to Laconia, but that didn't necessarily work," Campbell says. Center Harbor is a resort area across from Lake Winnipesaukeem while the Laconia gallery is in a downtown business district. "There are a lot of second homes on the lake, so we get a lot of weekend traffic," she says. "The Laconia store is in the downtown business district, so the people shop during their lunch hour and weekends are pretty slow. People look for bigger items in Center Harbor while they want more gift items in Laconia."

Market differences aside, having two shops is like having additional storage space for inventory, which can be a big plus if managed correctly. "It allows us, on certain lines, to carry more depth than we would have space for in one store," Diane Sulg says. What's more, slow sellers in one shop can find new eyes in the other, although, as she points out, "You have to be careful with that.

You can't overbuy with the premise that you can just move it to another store."

Inventory in both Maddi's Gallery locations is computerized using software which updates the database each night. "If someone says to us 'do you have this bowl in blue?' we can go on the computer and see if it's in stock at the other store," she explains. Another opportunity for efficiency is in special orders. Now, before an order is placed for one store, they check to see if the other gallery has the item in stock. Merchandise is transferred back and forth virtually every day. Diane and Madis Sulg spend most of their time in the original gallery, although one or the other visits the other store five days out of seven.

Secrets of success

- You don't have to go through a separate "learning curve" at each location

- You have experience with layout and display challenges

- Your accounting and point of sales systems are already in place

- Advertising can be handled by one person

- Sales materials such as bios can be maintained at a central location

- Ideas from shipping and packing to lighting, display, and sales techniques can be shared

- Customer service standards can be uniform

- Inventory can be moved between locations to accommodate for busy seasons at the various locations.

- Some ordering can be centralized

- Payroll and human resources can be centralized

- Computer systems can be networked

Campbell has two children, nine and twelve years old, and says running back and forth between her two stores is similar to the parenthood experience. "It's like having two kids going in opposite directions—you have to schedule yourself. We really rely on good help," she says. Yikes! has a staff of ten who all work in both locations so they know what's in stock at both stores. It also gives them a change of scenery, which is good for attitude.

One big benefit to operating multiple locations is the efficiency that comes from covering them all with the same advertising budget. Maddi's Gallery takes full advantage of that, promoting both stores at least twice a month in the local newspaper. They also advertise in two women's magazines, a city magazine, the Jewish news, a local travel magazine, an in-room hotel guide, and even occasionally in the New Yorker. In addition, they sponsor art fairs and other local events and use their 15,000-name customer list for direct mail, both traditional and email. As Madis explains, "We figured the advertising we do in the market would support both stores and we would get more bang for our buck that way."

Stress aside, there are several economic advantages to operating galleries in multiple locations. Simply being larger means you can spread direct expenses (like advertising and data processing) and some fixed overhead (like management salaries) over more revenue, improving your profit margin. Volume discounts—on everything from merchandise to telephone service—help margins, too, These will be offset somewhat by higher expenses in some areas, like gasoline for travel back and forth from one location to the other, but, on the whole, operating multiple galleries can be a rewarding experience.

"There is a challenge to setting up, to getting the systems worked out, but you can do it if you have bright, capable people," says Diane Sulg.

Extending the business

Just as home makeover programs are one of the hottest trends in reality TV, interior design services are major money makers for some art and craft gallery owners. But the interior design business isn't quite as simple as it seems on "Trading Spaces."

Lois Ross, who operates A Step Above Gallery & Interior Design Studio in the art district in Sarasota, FL, with her husband Shelly, loves the combination of businesses. An ASID (American Society of Interior Designers) member, Ross provides total design service, including lighting, walls, and flooring as well as kitchens. "When it's time for the furniture to go in, I select pieces from my gallery," she says. "We have paintings, we have gorgeous lamps, we have glass, wood, and very unusual objects. They're all art pieces, but they're furniture, too."

Her husband, Shelly, says they have 2,500 sq. ft. of retail space devoted to furniture and another 2,500 sq. ft. for the art and craft gallery. Displays are carefully mixed, however, to enhance the appeal of both.

"We do a couple of million dollars in design work," Lois Ross says with pride, but the business is not for the faint of heart. As a designer, she serves as general contractor for many jobs, overseeing the work of painters, electricians, and plumbers, flooring installers and other subcontractors. "I pay them and the client pays me," including a markup, she says. She gets a volume-based price from the subcontractors and marks it up to a price equal to what the homeowner would pay were they to hire the work done themselves.

Strictly a service

On a much smaller scale, Cindy Prieve of Studio 56 Art & Interiors in Waconia, Minnesota, offers color consulting and other design services to her gallery customers, primarily as a value-added service. "I offer it as a service to my clients to come into their homes to take a look at their space," she says. "I can make suggestions on accessories and/or paintings." Most compensation comes in the form of their artwork purchases. "I offer the service if I feel it's necessary to complete the sale, otherwise I charge a consulting fee."

Studio 56 was started by a group of female artists in 1998 and Cindy took it over a few years later. She is a multi-media artist who does a lot of work with found objects. The 1,600 sq. ft. shop sells pottery, jewelry, photography, paintings, and some clothing, all from Minnesota-based artists. "It's really more about the artwork. To me, design is just an added service that I can extend to the patrons."

Currently, design fees represent less than 10% of her gallery's revenues, according to Prieve, mainly because of time constraints. Prieve says she doesn't have time for many more than a couple of consulting jobs per month, especially since she is opening a second gallery location in a resort area: "It's not what I make my living off of. It's really more of a service to the patrons."

Patti Pegram took over Grey Gables Interior Design Studios in North Wilkesboro, NC, and added a craft gallery not long after when she bought a building that had enough space. Pegram has about 2,000 sq. ft. of retail space in the front of the building with another 2,000 for the design business in the back. She says she started the gallery because she really loves crafts, but also because, "It's hard to find really unique accessories for the jobs I work on. You basically come across just a lot of junk."

Cross-pollination

Two years ago, she gave the craft gallery its own name, Phases, to create a separate identity. The two businesses cross-pollinate, Pegram says: "Having Phases keeps people coming in the door and they see all the fabric samples and all the other things we offer. I have gotten quite a few jobs from people coming into the gallery."

Of course, gallery customers frequently look for free design services as well, which can be a tricky customer-relations situation. "I give a little bit of advice, then tell them I really don't have time and they'll need to make an appointment," Pegram explains. "I learned that through the years because I have given so much free advice on things and you think people will come back, but in the long run, they don't."

Having two revenue streams helps stabilize income, with the gallery contributing most heavily during the Christmas season and during their spring show, while the design business can be sporadic, depending on the projects going on at any given time. Gross sales are about equally divided, but the design business has a much higher profit margin. The interior design business isn't something to be started on a whim, though, according to Pegram. Sample books alone cost $12 to $15,000 yearly, she says, but you've got to have them. Fabrics, paint, window treatments, carpeting, furniture, all require samples on hand. But time is the biggest requirement. "I'm in and out constantly," she notes. That's why she has two full-time employees in the gallery as well an assistant that helps with the interior design business.

There aren't many legal restrictions to establishing an interior design business, although four states (Alabama, Louisiana, Nevada, Florida) as well as the District of Columbia and Puerto Rico require licensing and 17 others including New York, Illinois, and California, have voluntary registration or certification programs, according to Deana Waldron of the ASID. That's one reason the group estimates there are some 75,000 interior designers in the US.

Profits under glass

It sounds like perfect business synergy: the crafts gallery that does custom framing. But is it?

"They feed off of each other. People come in for gifts and they see that I have framing and then they come in for framing and they see that I have gallery items, so I couldn't have just a gallery and I couldn't have just a frame shop," says Margot Van Horn, Margot's Gallery & Frame in Oxford, MI. Van Horn's gallery, which features work from local artists, including sculpture, jewelry, pottery and glass, as well as wall art and decorative accessories, takes up two-thirds of her shop. The framing business, though, produces 75% of her sales.

Marie and Gary Perkins, who operate Finishing Touch Gallery in Fremont and Gallery On The Lake in Port Clinton, both Ohio, agree that framing encourages other purchases. "That's kind of one of our little marketing things inside the store," Marie says. "While we're figuring up the framing and putting everything into the computer, we encourage the customer to look around. We'll point out something new that has come in or something like that." She adds, "They have to bring their artwork in to design the framing and they also have to come back a second time to pick it up, so we've got two chances for them to walk through the store and to see what we have. If we're doing our job correctly, we point out other things in the store." Framing amounts to about half of their total business, which also includes glassware, pottery, jewelry, folk art, and sculpture, in addition to art prints.

But there are pitfalls, as well. While estimates of the size of the market range from $5 to $6 billion, there are some 20,000 custom frame shops in the United States, according to a widely-quoted industry figure, so competition can be fierce. There are also other considerations

Retailer or manufacturer?

Framing is very labor intensive and can be technically demanding. "Although it's not a physically hard thing to do, designing on the counter is probably the hardest thing to train because there is so much involved," Perkins says. "Every single piece that comes in is different and you have to really think about how am I going to attach this to the backboard, how deep of a frame do I need, what kind of spacing do I have to have."

Dennis Katayama, Katayama Framing in Portland, Oregon, points out another kind of space problem: "One of the things about the framing business is that it's kind of space intensive. To build the storage, to create enough space so that a painting can be handled properly and designed properly, and the frame executed properly, the space requirements are pretty horrendous. Most galleries' floor space and wall space is really needed for the artwork that they're showing."

You can't forget the equipment, either, Van Horn adds: "To start out, you need a glass cutter and a mat cutter and those can run $1500 apiece. You probably should get a dry-mount, and that's around $2500." You can also add some even more sophisticated technology to the operation. Computerized mat cutters, mat printing software for adding accents, and wood-working tools like double-cut miter saws and master-level joinery systems. Frame inventory isn't necessarily a problem, though, since there are "chop service" vendors that cut frame pieces to precise sizes that the gallery then assembles.

Clientele demands

Of course, there are also customers and their expectations. Perkins says 80% of framing is for pieces the customer brings in for that purpose, "It's everything from needlework to certificates and diplomas; artwork that maybe they buy on vacation. We do a lot of photographs. There are a lot of things that people get framed that most people don't even think about."

Van Horn adds, "I framed up a dried lizard one time. It was about six inches long, including the tail. We shadow-boxed it and framed it up on a suede matte."

Marilyn Murdoch, partner in Katayama Framing, says, "You have to deal with customers in an entirely different way. When our customer comes in, we start with what kind of home do you have: contemporary, antiques, craftsman? The last question I usually ask is how do you feel about the art? A gallery starts with that."

"My first feeling is that galleries should do well what they do well, and build a relationship with frame shops," Katayama says. "Find somebody they can feel comfortable with and work with and see eye-to-eye with to create a partnership that would be beneficial to both." He goes on to say that a sound model might be the gallery owner who works on frame design but hands over the execution to their frame shop partner. "The relationship with the customer then becomes better and closer and more controlled as opposed to sending customers all over the place," he says.

Perkins points out another pitfall: "There are other places you can go like Wal-Mart to buy an eight by ten frame, but people bring things to a custom framer because they are special, so they need to be treated that way. Everything has to be perfect. If you're not a perfectionist, you're not going to succeed in the framing business."

Chapter 31
Case Study: Selling Tangibles With Intangible Appeals
"Sound advice for selling exhaust systems
in the automotive aftermarket."

Who says bling-bling is a visual-only experience? If you sell performance exhaust systems, your customers are buying bling-bling for their ears, too, as well as extra horsepower for that flattened-against-the-seat feeling they get when they step on the accelerator. Appealing to all those senses is the key to selling more exhaust systems, according to marketers who specialize in the field.

"All of us men are the same," according to exhaust system manufacturer MBRP President Martin Barkey. "When you pull away from the stop sign and heads turn, that's worth the price of the exhaust system right there."

If you can make your customer imagine that experience in his or her ride, you're well along the way to selling them a new exhaust system. Explaining the technical advantages of T-304 stainless steel and full-mandrel bending is all well and good, but it's the sizzle that sells the steak, not the pedigree of the steer. When it comes to exhaust systems, it's the sound that sizzles.

That's why Flowmaster has more than thirty sound clips with BIG SOUND on its website, and Billy Boat Performance Exhaust has thirty-five videos with MORE BIG SOUND on its website.

"We're appealing to the senses," says Pete LaSacco, Director of Marketing. "When you put your foot on the accelerator, you're going to hear it. It's going to be louder and more muscular than the stock exhaust system. And you're definitely going to feel it."

Reach out to the customers

Getting the customer into the shop to consider an exhaust system upgrade is step one. "Stay in the public's eye," advises Barkey, whose company has been named one of Canada's fastest growing companies. "Go to the shows and let people see the product. See and be seen." But don't stop there, he continues. "Advertising goes hand-in-hand with the shows. People read the ads, then they see you at the shows and put a name to a face." That approach isn't only for national players, either, he says. "The dealers can put their ads in the local paper, display at the local fair or car show, and they'll be blown away when they see how their customers respond."

The main thing is to not wait and hope the customer finds you. You have to go out and get them, adds LaSacco.

It's essential to know your customer, too, and what factors influence their purchase decision. LaSacco observes, "The sports import market is very price conscious. They're very into what you can see, so my approach is to appeal to more senses. By restyling the underside of your car, you'll feel and hear the difference, although all you'll see are the tips." On the other hand, the premium car owner probably isn't concerned about the amount of bling-bling he's getting for his buck. "If the target market spends $50,000 on a car, they're not going to blink an eye about spending $1200 on an exhaust system," says LaSacco.

Flowmaster Executive Vice President Richard Small points out that, "One key is education. They need to learn more about our product line. We make about six hundred different items and most people don't even realize we make more than about two." He recommends, "When a customer comes through the door, you need to ask them what they really want. What are you looking for in the way of sound and performance? Too often, it's just a matter of 'do you have Flowmaster?' and the guy sitting there with a two-chamber will say 'sure' even though that's not probably not the right muffler for the customer."

Build your shop's selling skills

Dealer and distributor training is an important part of the equation for many manufacturers, and shop owners should be alert to such opportunities to improve their staff's product knowledge and selling skills. "We attend a lot of our wholesaler's open houses," reports Barkey. "We also meet with warehouse managers to train them on what we do."

Billy Boat's salespeople regularly meet with distributors to train their salespeople, too. "One problem is that there's a lot of turnover in the industry, so it's an on-going process," according to LaSacco. He adds that, for some makes, like Porsche, the amount of information the salesperson needs about the customer's ride is extensive. "The last thing you want to hear is that the handmade system the customer waited three weeks to get doesn't fit." Nobody wins in that one. It's up to the dealer to get the customer information right and manufacturer training helps him do that.

MBRP also invests a lot of manpower and money in technical assistance—and not just for the dealer's staff. "We allow our dealer's customers to call us direct for tech assistance," he explains. "We have techs sitting here to take those calls to help the customers bolt it on themselves. That's a big help to the dealers." He says they receive as many as 200 calls a day at their in-house tech-support center.

Flowmaster provides in-depth help on-line and in-person, according to Small. "One great educator is the company's website," he says. "They can check out what we have, they can check out the different sounds. We're constantly evolving as more and more customers are walking into stores asking for specific products." Their website includes installation videos and an 800 number for telephone access to the six gearheads standing by to help. "They speak the language," Small adds.

Use every marketing tool

Most manufacturers provide a wealth of sales tools to help the shop owner get their message across to the prospective customer. MBRP provides POP, banners, and brochures to bring their product to life. They're also working on a dealer co-operative advertising program to increase the exposure of their brand message. In addition, according to Barkey, "We produced an MBRP CD. Some use it for web sites, some use it for advertising in local magazines. It has hi-resolution images of vehicles we've built, some customer vehicles, a lot of write-ups on various part numbers. It also includes line drawings they can use or email to customers. Everything they need to move the product forward."

Billy Boat also provides logos, artwork, and other support material for websites. They try to work hand-in-glove with the dealer and distributor to keep product moving. "For some distributors, we actually do their catalog pages," reports LaSacco. They also provide tri-fold brochures specifically for targeted nameplates so that shop owners who specialize in Corvette work, for example, don't have to make their customers thumb through literature for Porsche and BMW.

Displaying exhaust products in the shop can be difficult, as Barkey points out: "The one negative to a full exhaust system is that it takes up a lot of real estate in a store, so brochures and banners help. Those customers with large stores that can display a complete system, it's pretty sharp."

Anticipate and overcome price objections

The most common obstacle to making a sale is pricing, according to most manufacturers. Unfortunately, not everyone can afford everything they want, so some potential customers aren't going to be converted to high-end systems. That's not all bad, though, because, as Barkey points out, "From the dealer standpoint, the lowest price doesn't always yield the best margin."

"Pricing is a big pitfall," he says. "You have to come back to the warranty, the performance gains, the 'fits right the first time.' We've tried to give good value for the money spent." That's good advice any time you're hearing a price objection from your prospect.

Quality, value, and, above all, head-turning sound are what sell performance exhaust systems, according to LaSacco. "If the dealers sell it on that basis, they'll enjoy success, too."

Chapter 32

Trade Show Exhibition For Fun And Profit

"Three P's—Planning, Preparation, and Presentation—combined with whole-hearted follow-up are your keys to getting the most out of your trade show marketing efforts."

Trade shows can be very effective outlets for showcasing your products and services to huge numbers of customers and potential clients. Most show attendees are there because they want to see how your product works and what it looks like while evaluating the competition. Most of them have some influence when it comes to purchasing for their company and surveys show that customers rate the importance of trade shows above trade magazine articles and regular sales contacts in terms of helping them make buying decisions.

As an exhibitor, you can use a trade show to strengthen existing business relationships, find new customers and potential partners, and scope out the competition.

Planning

Large companies can easily send people to a show without disrupting their operations, but for a small business owner, choosing which events to attend can be a difficult task. Going to a trade show not only costs money, it also can result in lost time running the business—a risk small business owners may hesitate to take. If you plan carefully, though, the opportunities to learn, grow and connect with other companies can outweigh the lost time and expense.

Success starts with identifying the right shows for your business. Check with your industry or trade association for scheduled shows that might be of interest. Consider everything from the location of the show to the after-hours parties. It goes almost without saying that the Internet will be a useful resource, too. If in doubt about whether a given show is going to be right for you, take a look at the list of exhibitors at past shows to see how many of your competitors are there. Program schedules can be helpful, too, by showing you what issues are of interest to the show's audience.

Here are several points to consider when choosing trade shows:

- Location. If any of your customers are located in the same city as the trade show, maximize your travel dollars by scheduling additional meetings or a visiting the client's office before or after the show.

- Exhibitors. Check for both competing firms and potential business partners or vendors. A trade show is a great opportunity to connect with new companies and check out your competition's products and services.

- Seminars. Look for learning opportunities for you and your staff that will help you acquire new skills or run your business more effectively. With careful scheduling, you can both man your booth and get in some cost-effective training. Seminars are also a great place to network!

- Keynotes. Big-picture sessions with guest speakers can provide insights into the trends and market forces that shape your industry and your business's future. Play your cards right and you can make some great contacts, too.

- Size. At a huge show, it's not as easy to navigate the floor or casually meet with other people; at a small show, you may not have as many opportunities to learn and network. But going to any show—big or small—will give you a chance to meet and talk face-to-face with key players and prospects.

- Parties. Networking is one of the most important reasons to attend a show, so choose those where you can arrange your schedule to attend dinners, cocktail hours and other opportunities where you can connect with your peers and potential business partners.

Preparation

Once you make your show selection, you'll need time to prepare for the opportunity. Before you do anything else, try to focus on what you hope to accomplish at the show. Is it to find new customers or build bonds with current ones? The type of display you have and the way you schedule your time will be affected by that simple decision. What's your budget? What about staffing? Travel? Do you need a booth design? Signage? Are you going to offer special promotions? Promote attendance with direct mail? Giveaways? Product demonstrations?

Make your decisions with return on investment in mind. High-tech displays and multimedia presentations are eye-catching but expensive, and they may not be as cost-effective as a couple of well-trained staffers armed with fact-filled sales brochures, a popular give-away item and a smile. Signage should be simple, direct and eye-level if possible, and should tout the benefits of your product or service, not just your name. Choose fewer and larger pictures rather than a lot of small ones. Spend a little time making a plan before you start making withdrawals from the company marketing budget.

Another big part of your preparation is pre-show promotion. If at all possible, get a copy of last year's attendance list for the show you're going to be in. A few weeks before the show, send a targeted mailing to prospects telling them about your company, your products and the people who can help them at your exhibit. If you can, include a floor diagram of the exhibit space, showing your location and your booth number. Point out bathrooms, pay phones, and entrances and exits to the building. Consider including a coupon or ticket that has to be turned in to receive a give-away item or to be admitted to a special briefing. The idea is to get prospects to remember who you are so they will make it a point to visit your booth.

Trade shows can also be a golden opportunity for your company to get media coverage, but that requires some advance work—sometimes far in advance. You don't have to be the biggest or the best company to get publicity, but you do have to be topical, different, informative and available. If you can find a way to emphasize any of those things, your chances of grabbing coverage will rise.

First, identify relevant trade media that cover your industry. If you haven´t contacted them before, this is a good opportunity to send a letter or press release with some background information about your company, your products, and what you´ll be doing at the trade show. Because most trade publications have lead times ranging from several weeks to several months, make contact as early as possible. Give other media, like daily and weekly newspapers, broadcast outlets, and web sites, several weeks' notice.

Try to schedule a new product introduction, update or other announcement to coincide with the show. Send a press release to the media with an "embargo" date to coincide with the show if you don't want the news to get out beforehand. And make the release do double duty by distributing it to your prospects too. If possible, coordinate your publicity efforts with the public relations efforts of the show´s organizers and ask if your media materials can be included in a press kit distributed by the show´s organizers.

Many shows are run by or otherwise connected with trade publications, which usually print a preshow edition. Check on advertising opportunities in the trade show edition of the host publication—and make sure the editors know about any news you´ll be making at the show. Promote your booth on your web site and consider banner ads for a short time on the sponsoring organization´s site or online magazine.

Look for a press room at the trade show where you can schedule a press conference to make announcements. Don't forget to stock the press room with press kits—and refresh the stock as necessary. Everything you distribute should have direct contact information for you, too, since many reporters will pick up your materials but not have time to contact you until after the show.

Don't ignore the local media. Did any of your executives graduate from a local college? Did they grow up in the area or have they worked there? A local angle is sometimes all it takes to get the local media´s attention. Don´t forget local television and radio, especially if you have a visually interesting product or if you can tie it in to something topical. Contact the station´s news director or editors who are in charge of making assignments for reporters. These days, nearly all media have web sites with contact information.

Weekly newspapers and business magazines are good media targets. Even small newspapers have business reporters who could write about your company if you can give them a reason to think their readers would be interested. Larger papers have reporters who cover specific businesses, industries or groups of industries. Contact them before the show to let them know about your participation.

Online publications and blogs are another opportunity to spread the word. Your trade show contact, trade association or industry group might help pinpoint online publications that plan coverage of the show.

Presentation

With the basics in place, turn to the specifics of your presentation. It's always helpful to sweat the details before you arrive at the trade show. Select the right people to staff your exhibit and give them some training in preshow meetings that specify goals and objectives. Agree on guidelines for interacting with visitors and qualifying customers. Explain what's expected both during show hours when the exhibit floor is open and at other times when customers and prospects may be looking for entertainment. You and your staff may be hoping for a little R&R during the show, but time spent on the golf course without a customer in your foursome is time wasted. Vacation on your own nickel, not the company's.

Pay attention to some common sense basics and prominently display company literature and give-away items at the back of your space so interested attendees will have to come inside to get them. Don't block the booth with tables, which can prohibit traffic flow into your area. If you have room to set aside a space for one-on-one conversations, separate it from the rest of the booth with a curtain for privacy. Consider hosting a cocktail party or special event for current customers—and invite them to bring their friends.

Sales from trade shows come from your ability to get qualified leads and convert them into purchasers. Trade show selling is slightly different than other sales methods, but it's not complicated.

Start the process by preselling your booth to customers and prospects by sending them a note or an email with your booth number, inviting them to stop by and pick up a small gift, participate in a giveaway or take advantage of special show prices. If they respond positively and want to buy at the show, be sure to have a separate location (or at least a quiet spot in the back of the booth) where you can close the sale.

Sales fundamentals still apply. The more prospects you see, the more sales you will make, so contact all the visitors you can. Develop a short list of questions to quickly separate the serious buyers from the browsers. Focus on the buyers. Prepare a thirty-second "elevator speech" that highlights the benefits of using your products or services. Get contact information and then move on to the next prospect. Buyers are busy, too, and they'll appreciate your cordial efficiency.

If you sense a big prospect with serious interest, be prepared. If you can afford it, rent a hotel suite to entertain small groups of VIP prospects. Invite qualified prospects for cocktails, dinner or perhaps breakfast the next morning. The object is to spend quality time with those prospects who are most likely to place large orders.

Because trade shows pack a bunch of opportunity into only a few days, the pressure can be intense and the hours long. That means you need enough people to work the exhibit and the ability to rotate your staff to keep them fresh. Upbeat people with stamina make good booth staffers. You'll also need staffers to man the booth while you deal with the biggest prospects yourself.

One of the best reasons to attend trade shows is to gather competitive information—and some of the best comes from customers. That's one of the many good reasons to talk to as many people as possible at the show. Every prospect has information you need, even if they don't want or need your products. What are they interested in? Who do they buy from? Why? How much do they buy? When? At what price? The answers don't have to result in a sale to be valuable.

If you see your competitors´ materials in a visitor's hands, ask them what they think of the company, its people and products. How do their prices compare? It never hurts to hear what prospective customers think is important. Also, people like to be asked their opinion because it makes them feel important. You´ll be surprised at just how much information some people are willing to share. Ask and they´ll probably tell you.

You're at the show to make contact. You can scope out new and existing competitors, partner with allies, and even shop for suppliers—all by listening to what the visitors to your exhibit tell you.

Follow-up

As soon as practical, hold a post-show debriefing to let everyone share what they heard and learned. Get commitments from staff on their follow-up plan for every lead generated during the show. Those leads, and your resulting sales, are the real payoff from an effective trade show performance.

Not every sale occurs at the show. Sometimes buying cycles are spread out over many months, so follow-up is essential to capturing those orders. Find a way to stay in touch with your show prospects. A letter or card might work. With email so prevalent, a monthly electronic newsletter featuring your latest product information, new prices or new services can become as easy to produce as pushing a few buttons on your computer—if you have a current contact list.

As soon as you return from the show, send a follow-up letter to the entire mailing list to whom you announced your booth before the show. Then send qualified leads you gathered at the show a more complete follow-up mailing package that doesn't just duplicate the information you gave them at the booth. Finally, there's no substitute for the old-fashioned telephone call. It's the most powerful post-trade show marketing follow-up, and you should be sure to call every lead contacted at the event.

Finally, don't forget the media after the show. Did you make a big deal with a new or existing customer at the show? Announce it! Do you have some quotes (get some if you don't) from customers who commented on your new products at the show? Tout them! Even a press release talking about how pleased you were with the show can be newsworthy for someone—including the show's organizers, who may include it in their own press material or web site.

An investment in trade show marketing is a sound one. Increase the return on your investment by planning to attend the best shows for your company, preparing yourself, your staff, and your customers and prospects, and presenting your products and services in ways that take advantage of the trade show environment. With solid, consistent follow-up, you'll reap the rewards.

Chapter 33
Getting The Most Out Of Attending Trade Shows
"Set goals and manage your time to maximize the return on your trade show investment."

At a typical Las Vegas trade show, you can walk eleven miles, shake hands with 80,000 people, and listen to 4,000 sales pitches. When you try to do it all, it's exhausting, chaotic, and mind-boggling. Or it can be exhilarating, profitable, and informative. Like any other day in your business, the results depend largely on your attitude and actions.

To get the most out of your trip, set some goals for the show. Making the million-dollar pull on the dollar slot may be your hope, but you probably have some more serious reasons for going. Trade shows primarily serve as information-gathering events, so your goals will center on learning about the many factors that affect your business.

Why are you going?

Seeing vendors and their product lines is almost always number one on the list but your goal should be a little more specific than "seeing suppliers." Decide whom you're going to see and whether you will do any actual buying at the show or just gather information for future orders.

Another goal is to keep up with industry developments and customer preferences. Specificity is key. You shouldn't go just to "see what's happening." Is there a new product category emerging? Are customers in other parts of the country dong things differently? You'll have your own ideas about which areas to pursue, but ask your staff as well.

Finding out what the competition is up to may be another important goal. Are any of the mass retailers stepping up activity? Are they increasing product lines or adding locations? Your competition from across the street may be at the show, too, so asking the vendors a few discrete questions might prove productive.

Getting a "Las Vegas education" usually means losing your shirt at the craps table. During a trade show, though, you can choose from dozens if not hundreds of seminars, workshops, and product demonstrations, so consider setting aside some time to improve your business or technical skills while you're there.

Some of the other goals you may want to set include finding potential employees, strengthening vendor or customer relationships, or exploring partnerships or investment opportunities.

Choosing your specific goals will lead naturally into a list of questions to ask at the show. Write them down! It may seem like overkill, but having a written list will be invaluable in the middle of the hubbub on the show floor.

What are your priorities?

Once your goals are determined, draw up a plan of attack. During a typical four-day show, the show floor is open thirty-one hours. If you tried to visit every booth, you'd have to stop at one every ten seconds. So, with the show schedule and exhibitor list in hand, make a list of "Must See" and "Like To See" exhibits.

Then allot some time (including travel) to each one. A visit to a vendor to negotiate a deal should probably take twenty minutes. If you are going to comparison shop that vendor's competition, allow the same for each one. For information-only visits, count on half that amount depending on how many questions you have on your list.

You need to set aside some time (about 35%) for unexpected opportunities, travel between the convention center and your hotel, as well as lunch and other breaks. Assuming you attend the entire show, you will have about twenty hours on the floor for planned visits and eleven for contingencies.

Then choose your seminars and social events. You'll have to make some hard choices, because there are concurrent workshops as well as numerous product demonstrations! There are also a dozen social events, some held during exhibit floor time.

Make appointments

The final time-management step before leaving for the show is the one most trade show attendees ignore—making appointments. Call every "Must Have" exhibitor and set a specific time to meet for the appropriate ten or twenty minutes. Set these meetings for between 10 AM and 4 PM, leaving the first and last exhibit hours open. Since the show covers more than a million square feet, you'll probably want to group your meetings geographically so have the exhibit hall maps in hand when you make the calls.

Why should you go to this trouble? Because it puts you in control of your time. Assuming you spend five nights in Las Vegas, your investment in hotels, airfare, and other travel expenses can total more than $3,000. That means every one of the thirty-one hours on the floor costs nearly $100—not including the value of your time. How much time do you want to spend waiting around a booth for a sales rep or technician? Having a schedule to follow also keeps you more focused on the business at hand.

Show time

Your badge is pinned on and through the doors you go, ears and eyes open, notepad at the ready.

When you made your appointments, you kept the first and last hours of the show floor day open. Those hours are the ones when traffic is lightest, so you can get to more exhibits and receive more attention when you get there. It's a good time to see people you couldn't get appointments with or to explore some of the "Like To See" exhibits.

When you enter an exhibit, it's important to manage the conversation. Minimize the small talk and ask your questions. If the sales rep starts a pitch about something unrelated to your needs, cut it off with one of your questions. What if the person you want to see is talking to someone else? Use a polite elbow (figuratively speaking) by standing near enough to overhear them. At an appropriate opening, tell them that you're interested in the same thing they're discussing and ask a question. Most of the time, the first person will wrap up their business quickly and leave the exhibitor to you. If someone tries to cut in on you, by the way, just keep focused and make sure your questions get answered first.

Your overriding goal is to get information, but that doesn't mean you need to carry tons of it around with you. Every exhibitor will try to press literature into your hands. Don't take it unless it's really important to you now. Instead, ask the rep to send it to you after the show. Keep that tactic in mind when you're standing in line to get that imprinted combination screwdriver-bolt cutter-juice squeezer, too. Do you want to carry that around with you all day?

Many times, you'll ask a question the exhibitor can't answer and they'll promise to get back to you with the information after the show. To make sure they do, write your question on your business card and give it to them. Do the same with their card when they give it to you. Now there's no excuse for either one of you to forget to follow up later. You can also get the name of the engineer or technician the exhibitor is going to ask—then call them yourself.

Workshops and networking

If you attend a workshop, take a checklist of questions—then ask them at the first opportunity. Assuming you have time at the end of the presentation, move to the speaker's vicinity and listen to other questions—or ask your own. If you find that you're sitting through a workshop that's not going to be useful, leave quietly and find a more productive way to use your time.

Exhibitors don't have a monopoly on useful information. Your peers (the other 79,999 attendees) face the same issues and have the same concerns you do. The most useful information you pick up may come from someone in a market across the country.

Networking opportunities include everything from scheduled social events to shuttle bus rides. Catch someone's eye, ask him or her a question, and then introduce yourself. Ask them which exhibit impressed them the most or what new product they consider the hottest.

At the end of the day you should have a pocket bulging with business cards and a pad full of notes. Take a few moments to review them to see if there's anything that needs follow-up while you're at the show. You might want to highlight items you need to address when you get home. It's easier to decipher your notes while they're fresh in your mind. Some people also code the business cards they've picked up, marking them as vendors, prospects, or competitors.

The show doesn't end when you head for McCarran International Airport. There are four things you should do as soon as you get back. First, confirm in writing any deals that you made during the show. The rep may have a fantastic memory, but details tend to get lost. Second, brief your staff on what you learned at the show. Third, update your contact files with all those business cards. Finally, do an honest post mortem to determine whether the time, effort, and money you just invested will give you an adequate return. Did you accomplish your goals? Is there anything you'll do differently next year?

Then start packing for the next show.

Chapter 34
Trade Show Seller Secrets
"A trade show is a great place to make good deals, especially if you know how the seller's mind works."

Do you feel like a mackerel when you walk into the convention exhibit halls at a trade show? It seems like there are hundreds of anglers aiming to hook your checkbook and sharks trying to take a bite out of your wallet. In other words, there are sellers in every exhibit working to get your business.

If you know what those sellers are thinking and what they're going to do next, you'll be a much more effective buyer. Here's a look at what's going on in the sales rep's head and some tips on how you can bring home the best deals. Several factors affect the process, most of which give you an edge.

Trade show buying factors

Time is the biggest factor for both the buyer and the seller. The sales rep is under pressure to sell as many prospects as possible in the thirty-one hours the floor is open. You can always skip an event to gain some time, but the rep needs to make every minute count. On the other hand, you don't have time to play "hard to get." This is a good negotiating ploy under normal conditions, but is generally a waste of time at a trade show. If you intend to be a buyer, say so.

Information and who has it is another factor. You know how big an order you expect to place, but the rep doesn't. You know what the competition has offered; the rep doesn't. It's the seller's job to pry this information out of you and, to serve your own ends, you'll probably give some of it up—but you control the flow.

Then there's the turf factor. The convention hall lobbies, restaurants, and aisles are yours. When you step into an exhibit, though, you're on the seller's turf. They outnumber you. They know the staff, have access to the private rooms, and control the key to the freebie vault. The offsetting advantage you have, of course, is that you can escape at any time.

Buy-Sell transaction stages

Most buy-sell transactions occur in stages. The first thing the typical salesperson will do is try to qualify you. The time factor is at work here, since the trade show seller wants to deal only with those prospects that intend to buy today or in the near future. You will be asked a few questions to determine whether you are a tourist, a tire-kicker, or a buyer. A tourist is just passing through. They may be a "layperson" that is an enthusiastic hobbyist but doesn't work in the industry. When asked if they need some help, a tourist will say "No thanks—just looking" or something to that effect. Unless you want to waste time tracking down a sales person later, avoid these types of phrases.

A tire kicker is someone who won't buy right now but may in the future. A rep will want to spend only as much time as it takes to get contact information for future follow-up and hand you a brochure. If an immediate buyer walks into the exhibit, the seller will drop the tire kicker and go to pursue today's order. To keep the salesperson's attention, imply that you might place an order today and ask plenty of questions to display your interest. You may have to deal with the rep's attempts to close a sale, but that's easily handled by saying "No." Finally, don't just give the sales rep your card when you leave. Get his or hers, too, and give them a specific time to contact you. It's only fair that you give them some hope of a sale after you've taken up their time.

You will be the center of attention, of course, if you tell the seller you're there to place an order. As mentioned earlier, negotiating games are time wasters so it's best to get right down to business. When you're qualified as a buyer, you enter the needs analysis stage of the process. The salesperson will want to know several things about you beginning with whether you are the final decision maker or a decision influencer who will make recommendations to someone else. The decision maker will get a little stronger closing effort, but either one should receive full attention.

What do you need?

Among other things, the rep should try to determine your needs for his or her product line. Is it replacing an existing line or are you restocking? Are you adding a new line? Do you want to upgrade to a higher price point or expand your offerings? In other words, what you trying to accomplish by making this purchase? The seller will also want to know the potential size of your order, of course, as well as when you intend to place it. A good salesperson will probe to find your "hot buttons," or the criteria like price, delivery date, terms, etc., that you will use to make a decision.

The temptation is great to play games during this stage—to withhold information or play hard-to-get. You may want to stall for time later (see below), but it's best to cooperate now. After all, you need to qualify the seller and product line, too. The best way to find out if they can satisfy your needs is to be very specific about what you're looking for and why you want it. The only factor you might fudge on is the order size. It's generally a good idea to imply that you're going to place a monster order so you'll be offered the best price and terms.

The third stage comes when the seller starts pitching his line. Unfortunately, too many reps have been trained to push their company's newest product regardless of what the customer actually needs. This is a huge time-waster, so don't hesitate to interrupt and ask them to present only the lines that meet your needs. It's your money on the table so you're in charge.

When the seller offers a product you like, be straightforward about any obstacles that might prevent you from buying it. Don't offer objections just for the sake of objecting. Instead, make sure you're very clear about what information you still need. It is your responsibility to learn everything you need to know to make an informed purchase—and the rep's to provide it.

The end game

The seller at some point will ask for the order. This isn't the end of the buy-sell process, but it's the beginning of the end. There are dozens of different tactics the salesperson may use, ranging from a direct question ("Do you want to buy this?") to the alternatives close ("Do you want us to ship by ground or air?"). If you have all the product information you need, this signals it's time to enter the negotiation stage.

One of the great advantages of buying at a trade show is the huge number of vendors to choose from. Any given product category will probably have dozens of vendors and suppliers competing for your business. Ask the rep that's trying to close you for the offer in writing, and then go see his competitors. If he won't put it in writing, take notes yourself and confirm the details with him before you leave. That way you know you're comparing apples to apples and he knows he better offer you the best price right now—you may not be back otherwise.

Once you've done your comparison shopping, go to the supplier you've chosen and move into the final stage, placing the order. Here you can use all the factors—time, information, and turf—to your advantage. Begin by asking the rep if his previous offer is as good as he can do. Tell him or her you've gone to X number of his competitors and you want to review the offers before making a final decision. Don't report a fictitious counter-offer, since a good seller will know the competition's price range and detect a bluff.

Stand near an exit from the exhibit to signal your willingness to walk away. Keep the escape option open especially if the seller takes you into a "closing room" and/or calls over a manager to help close the deal.

Try to take up some more of the seller's time, since the more of it is invested in you, the greater the urge to close the sale. Finally, make an offer you'd be comfortable accepting (not a ridiculously low one—that may blow the work you've done) and ask to place the order right now. You'll be surprised how often your offer is accepted. And the worst that can happen is you get the original deal, which your shopping has shown to be the best anyway.

A trade show is a great place to make good deals, especially if you know how the seller's mind works. You can shop among dozens of competing vendors, see new equipment and supplies, watch product demos, and do hands-on testing. You may even pick up a free T-shirt or two to go with your great buy.

Section Five
Family Business Strategies

Dilemmas and dramas are inherent in family businesses. Managing a company with family members as part of the workforce creates endless conflict while separating family demands from company needs can be nearly impossible. This section uses ten case studies to examine issues from hiring family members to planning for transition of ownership to the next generation.

Family businesses confront the same problems faced by any small company—and then some. Squabbles over titles and responsibilities get confused with sibling rivalries while adapting to changing market conditions often conflicts with cherished tradition. The very real family-owned companies in this section represent a cross-section of enterprises passed down from generation to generation. In every one, they've faced down the demons of family involvement and built growing, successful companies.

Chapter 35
The Family Business Soap Opera
"Family dynamics add drama
to everyday management decisions"

"Hey Dad! Can I take the company out for a spin?"

It's not hard to imagine a family business founder hearing those words. Nor is it difficult to feel the patriarch's gut-wrenching reaction. He slaved for years building a successful business, creating a product, toiling to find customers, striving to beat the competition. How in the world can he entrust his life's work to that kid who once vomited in his lap on the roller coaster at Coney Island?

Such dilemmas and dramas are inherent in family businesses as they pass (or not) from generation to generation. In addition to finding good employees, the family business owner has to somehow fit his or her offspring, cousins, and in-laws into the workforce. Without destroying morale. Or the business. He or she has to not only mediate customer complaints but somehow separate siblings whose rivalry makes the Yankees-Red Sox look like a love fest. And should he fire daughter Susie's ex-husband before or after the divorce is final? Or not at all?

"Usually, family business problems have less to do with money and more to do with the roles of family members," according to consultant Joe Pastore, Professor Emeritus and former University

Provost at Pace University's Lubin School of Business. "The root of most problems is the role conflict between family position and business position. It's extremely difficult to separate the two."

Or, as White Plains, NY, attorney Andrew Karlen, who has specialized in family business matters for 35 years points out, "The business is the business and Thanksgiving dinner is Thanksgiving dinner."

Karlen says family dynamics are almost inevitably intertwined with how the business is run. " I was meeting with a family management team once," he says, "and the dad took me across the hall to show me how messy his son's office was. You'd think he was showing me a teenager's bedroom at home." Normal business relationships become complicated when family is involved, he adds. "I may work at the family company and have ownership, while my brother may be CEO and also have ownership. We both may get dividends, but I'm not entitled to the same salary just because my last name is the same." Sibling rivalry, anyone?

The dynamics of managing employees are different in a family-owned business, too. "Let's face it," Pastore says, "family members are treated differently than non-family members. Most employees recognize a slight sense of injustice there. You can't tell a non-family employee they better stop coming in late, for example, when a family member gets away with it."

Such issues face a surprisingly large number of companies, although the exact number depends on how you define a "family business." Some estimates are as high as 90% of all US businesses, but those include every sole proprietorship in the country, many of which won't be passed to the next generation.

Ed Rosenfeld was president of one such family business, International Furniture Rentals in Hawthorne, NY, until it was sold to Warren Buffet's Berkshire Hathaway. Today he serves as a consultant to other family-owned businesses and has seen plenty of role confusion in them. "If there are other family members in the business, their relationships with the founder are fraught with emotion. The founder may not always be aware of when he or she is functioning as father or mother, boss, or investor." He adds, "They are often fearful of conflict and so are frozen in inertia or are caught in a conflict that is destructive to the business."

Given all this *sturm und drang*, how can family businesses survive from one generation to the next?

Many don't. The Family Firm Institute estimates that only 30% of US family firms survive the shift to the second generation, only 12% are still viable in the third generation and only 3% make it to the fourth generation or beyond. Of course, not all of the firms actually fail; many are sold to buyers outside the family or simply stop operating because they were sole proprietorships whose owners don't have heirs. Still, family businesses face some unique issues.

In a 2010 survey by PriceWaterhouseCoopers, 44% of family business owners said they'd quarreled about the future direction of the business, and 36% that they had argued about the performance of family members employed in the company. Every consultant I talked to recommended the company form an advisory board to provide advice and outside perspective. "It's important to have people who are respected and bring skills to the table," Karlen says. "The company lawyers and accountants are paid advisors anyway, so they really shouldn't be on that board. People in similar non-competing companies, retired business people, or even people with connections might be very valuable."

Then there is the question of hiring family members. "Is every member of the family automatically entitled to work at the company?" Karlen asks. "That may not be a good idea." Companies should require family members to have a college education and outside work experience before they join the business, according to Karlen. He says that not only improves the quality of their work, but gives the individual a better sense of accomplishment and self-worth. He adds, "It's also a good idea to have them report to someone other than their own father."

As Rosenfeld explains, "Any business has to be able to recruit and retain good employees. You have to recruit a family member into the business with open eyes." After all, "One of the advantages of being an entrepreneur is creating a nice situation for your children, but if that's the only criterion for hiring a family member, the other employees won't respect that person." In addition to an advisory board, he recommends a mentoring system, where a non-family employee works with the new hire to ensure equitable treatment. He points out, "The family member shouldn't be at the whim and mercy of their parent."

"The message to the family has to be that they have no special privileges," Pastore adds. "The non-family employees have to know they have the same rights and obligations."

Succession is the biggest question of all, of course. "There's always the issue of whether dad or mom are ready to let go. And if they are, do they really let go?" according to Karlen. "You can't just appoint a successor, you have to anoint one. The employees have to know who is really in charge and making the decisions."

But who gets the big job? The oldest son? The hardest-working daughter? "Everyone thinks succession is clear cut—I'm entitled to be next!" Karlen points out. "Honesty and openness are critical. Having independent board members can also take some of the burden off the owner. A child may not be qualified to be CEO, but could be great in some other capacity like marketing or sales."

Pastore adds a philosophical overview of family business dynamics: "You start out by being nice to one another but there may come a time when there's some push back, so you have to have the strength to stand up to it. The most important thing is a commitment to a long-term relationship from both the business standpoint and the family."

In the end, he adds, "Sometimes you have to make a choice between family and business. Would you really sacrifice your family to keep the business?"

Chapter 36
Case Study: Changing Direction
From Generation To Generation
"It was almost like we were thrown into the deep end.
I was 22 at the time."

Changing direction is hard for any company, but it can be particularly trying for a family business—especially one dominated by a patriarch for forty years. That was the case at Wilson & Son Jewelers, the Scarsdale, NY, institution that's been in business since 1905.

"When Mike and I came into the business, it was on life support," says Matt Wilson, great-grandson of the company founder. "If you were to walk into our Scarsdale store in 1985, you'd have seen the same paint, floor, and ceiling as in 1940. The problem was that people were going to the nice new shiny stores. Finally, my father, Ira, put his foot down and rebuilt the store."

Blocking change had been Meyer Wilson, son of the founder, Morris Wilson, and a believer in projecting a less-than-prosperous image. "My grandfather's philosophy was that you didn't want to drive a nice car or look too successful because customers would think you were overcharging." The Wilsons today don't think that way, according to Matt. "I like to do business with people who are successful." He believes his customers do, too.

An even bigger change, though, was the way decisions were made when Matt and Mike's father, Ira, took over the company. "The pendulum swung just the other way," Matt Wilson says. "Whereas my grandfather wouldn't let my father make any decisions, my father just told Mike and me to 'go for it.' It was almost like we were thrown into the deep end. I was 22 at the time."

The two brothers decided to jump on the branded merchandise trend that was developing in the jewelry trade at the time. Today, Wilson & Son is the exclusive dealer for Rolex in Westchester County and handles dozens of other major name brands as well. The company also handles repairs and appraisals and has three gemologists on the staff of fourteen. In 2006, they added a store in Mount Kisco, NY. In 2011, the company was inducted into the Westchester Business Council Hall of Fame.

The future undoubtedly holds more transformation for Wilson & Son, but an ownership change isn't likely, according to Matt, who is 45. His brother, Mike is 47 and their father, Ira, is a young 72 and still very involved in the business. There are a total of eight grandchildren in the wings. "They'd have to work somewhere else for a couple of years first," Wilson explains. "But they'd have to really appreciate what they have here. It's open to them, but not a sure thing." On the other hand, he says, "The thought of selling the business just isn't appealing to us. The company has been around since 1905 and we're helping third generation customers!"

Chapter 37
Case Study: Growth Through Family Ownership
"They feel very good about the fact that we're a family business."

Propane distributor Paraco Gas leaped from $1.8 to $100 million in annual sales in a little over 40 years largely on the strength of family ownership. Company founder Pat Armentano started selling welding supplies from a garage in Mount Vernon, NY, in 1968, but he and his sons grew it by acquiring more than twenty other mostly family-owned propane companies over the years. For the acquired companies, selling to another family-owned business made the transaction more palatable.

Today, the company has about 300 employees and 80,000 customers from Virginia to Massachusetts who buy propane for residential heating, cooking, hot water, and recreational uses like pool heat and outdoor grills. They also supply Home Depot and other retailers in the metro NY region through a tank exchange program.

It's a very fragmented market. The nation's top ten propane companies combined only control about 35% of it, with about 3,000 little companies dividing up the rest. When it comes time for the small independent to sell their business, Paraco steps in. "We're very competitive in that area," says CEO Joe Armentano. "They feel very good about the fact that we're a family business. We keep their employees, their customers, we try to be part of the local community. We relate very well with the small independent." The company's own roots go a long way toward building trust, Armentano says. Typically, Paraco keeps the acquired company's name for about a year, then combines it with "Paraco" for a couple of years more, finally changing to the Paraco brand after the transition.

Joe Armentano, 57, worked alongside his father (who passed away in 2010) and took over as CEO in 1988. His youngest brother, John, 47, is VP for acquisitions and development. There are two other brothers who aren't with the company.

Working with family members hasn't always been ideal. "When you get into family situations, it can be challenging to make sure everyone is part of a team," Joe Armentano says. "You have to separate the family relationship from the business relationship. At one time we had a cousin in the business that I had to fire. It was tough to see him a week later at a family picnic."

Aside from their first venture from welding supplies into the propane business itself, which occurred in 1979, the event that really shaped the company's future was in 1985, when they borrowed heavily to buy two Suburban Propane locations on Long Island. "That prompted me to go back to school to get an MBA in corporate finance," Armentano says. He added the advanced degree to his business degree from Fordham University. That acquisition also necessitated adoption of more of a corporate culture. He explains, "We went from the typical mom-and-pop family environment to having a professional management team, audited statements, bank loans, etcetera."

Armentano hopes to double the company's size in the next five years, but he says that won't mean a change from family ownership, although the third generation may or may not be involved in management. "Being privately held, we can drive the culture the way we want to drive it," he says. "You can stay true to the values you personally want to have. You also have an environment where employees look at it as something more than just a job—they're part of something that's growing."

Chapter 38

Case Study: Family Ownership But Not Family Management
"They entrusted day-to-day management
to non-family executives."

The Muselman family has owned Indiana's Design Resource Group for more than 80 years. But since the late 1990s, they have entrusted its day-to-day management to non-family executives, re-defining their role as owner-investors rather than owner-operators. Here's how they made the transition.

Dynamic Resource Group, a Berne, Ind., publisher of magazines, books and catalogs for needlecrafters and other hobbyists, was founded in 1925 by German-born immigrant Chris Muselman. Today the company, known as DRG, is still wholly owned by the Muselman family. But since the late 1990s, DRG has been managed entirely by non-family executives.

DRG's third-generation co-owners—cousins Roger Muselman, 42, the chairman of the board, and Tom Muselman, 48, the president—say they haven't withdrawn from the business; they've just adjusted their sights to focus on the larger issues. "We're flying at 40,000 feet instead of crop-dusting," Roger explains.

The Muselmans shifted their role from owner-managers to owners-as-investors in stages, not in one big reorganization. They tried a few different systems, talked to numerous experts and finally arrived at an arrangement they characterize as "noses in, fingers off." As Roger Muselman explains it, "The day-to-day is in someone else's hands, but the governance is not."

DRG's individual publications may serve small markets, but the company is no seat-of-the-pants operation, with annual sales of about $70 million, 50 revenue streams, 300 employees and annual growth exclusive of acquisitions of 10%.

But is DRG still a "family" business?

"In the old days, people used to think that if a company wasn't family-run, it wasn't a family business. Today, that isn't necessarily the case," says Scottsdale, AZ-based family business consultant Leslie Dashew, who helped counsel the Muselman family through their transition. A more important question, perhaps, is: Does such a move make the business—and the family—stronger or weaker?

"The business should be an asset that the family owns, instead of the business owning the family," Dashew says. "The importance of the business is not necessarily to provide employment for the family, but to provide a return. That's the psychological shift of thinking of the business from the standpoint of investors."

Dashew says a family should consider four factors when transitioning from owner-managers to owner-investors.

1. Family Vision: The family needs a shared vision for the role the business plays in their lives.

2. Asset Attitude: The business should be regarded as an economic asset like any other to be bought, sold, invested in, grown or preserved.

3. Outside Directors: Effective directors provide oversight to ensure the business is being run properly.

4. Communication Link: If you don't have structures to make sure communication happens, you risk a lot of problems.

Above all, Dashew says, "Communication is the currency of family business. You need a good management team, a good board of directors, and a family council of some kind." Family members, she says, must meet "to talk about what they want and what's going on, whether or not they are an owner."

Tom and Roger Muselman teamed up to develop a plan for the transition a few years after the two of them started filling their fathers' shoes in management. "We soon understood," Tom says, "that if we were going to take this company to the next level, we were going to have to step back and, instead of being owner-operators, we had to become owner-investors. We had to find people who had the competencies to take us to the next level."

The two men serve on the company's board of directors but stay out of day-to-day operations. "We've got really, really smart people who grow our company organically," Roger explains. "In addition, because of our structure, we have Tom and I, our board members, and our CEO who can look at acquisitions and new opportunities. If we didn't have the structure we have, we'd all just be working on the project of the day."

The structure also allowed the company to weather a string of tragic losses. Former CEO John Robinson, who joined DRG in 1985 and worked closely with the family to create the management structure, died of cancer at age 60 in 2006. Carl Muselman, Tom's father and part of the second-generation duo that laid the foundation for the company's success, passed away at age 78 in 2006 and not long afterward, Gary Richardson, 56, editorial director for the company, died unexpectedly as well. While the board conducted an extensive search for a new CEO and the family dealt with their personal losses, Tom and Roger stepped up to help interim CEO David McKee run the company. After a nationwide search, McKee was named permanently to the CEO's post.

Growth and complexity

Chris Muselman, who started the company—originally named Economy Printing—eventually became a lawyer and lost interest in the small business, according to his son Art, who bought it with his brother, Carl, in 1959. At that time, it was an $80,000-a-year operation.

The brothers divided the responsibilities along with the equity on a 50/50 basis. "We worked together well for over 40 years," explains Art, 76. "The thing that made it work was that we had our job descriptions completely separated. Carl ran the production and purchasing; I did all the selling, credit and collections, and finances." He adds with a chuckle, "I got the money in and he spent it out."

Over time, two things changed for Carl and Art: Both their business and their families grew. In 1985, they bought the House of White Birches, a publisher of niche magazines. It was the first of a string of acquisitions that eventually included Annie's Attic, the American School of Needlework, Needlecraft, and Clotilde, all publishers of books, magazines catalogs, and other material serving the craft and cooking markets. A separate subsidiary, Strategic Fulfillment Group, provides database marketing and fulfillment services from a 140,000-square-foot facility in Big Sandy, Texas.

It didn't take long for the publishing companies to eclipse the printing business, which created a tail-wagging-the-dog situation. Carl's son, Tom, had joined the printing company in a full-time plant operations role in 1980. Art's son, Roger, started in printing sales in 1986. The boys' responsibilities in the family business grew, but they remained tied to the printing business; publishing operations were managed by executives either acquired along with the companies they bought or recruited for their expertise in the field.

Carl and Art were approaching their sixties and thinking about retirement and succession plans. Passing the equity along to the next generation was relatively easily arranged through grantor retained interest trusts, which eventually made Tom and his brother John (who died in 2004) equal partners with Roger and his sister Karen. The sticky point was management succession.

"We were trying to make a co-CEO-thing between Roger and Tom, but that didn't resonate with either Carl or I," Art explains. "We didn't know which one to pick. We also figured it was too big for either one of the boys to be CEO. I also don't know that they really wanted it."

The cousins had their differences, too, according to Roger. "Tom was handling manufacturing and I was handling sales," Roger recalls. "He would always say we could make more money if I brought in more sales, and I would always say that we could make more sales if we could produce a quality product on time. When you start going down that path, you see that we could end up like many family businesses. We decided to step above this to preserve our friendship and to preserve our company."

Outside help was the key to the transition. Both generations started investing their time and money in family business seminars at nearby Goshen College, hired an array of family business consultants, legal advisers, and financial planners, and studied their next moves carefully. "The Muselmans never chinch on advice," Art explains. "You better know what you can do and what you can't do.

Another key player in the transition was the late John Robinson, then CEO of the publishing companies, who joined the family as chief executive officer of House of White Birches in 1989 and spearheaded the publishing acquisitions over the years. Robinson was named CEO of DRG in 1998.

But it was Tom and Roger who really drove the transition from family-as-managers to family-as-investors, according to Mike Cohn, managing director of CFG Business Solutions in Phoenix, one of the family business consultants intimately involved with the process. "We helped them form an ownership team so Art and Carl could feel comfortable about having them step up," Cohn says. They were joined in the process by Roger's sister Karen and Tom's brother John.

"The four cousins felt that the businesses were so complex and the competition was so tough, that they wanted smarter people to run the businesses for them than they could do themselves," Cohn says. "They were pretty insightful about their own limitations. They were also passionate about their ownership. It was a legacy asset, and they had a real sense of stewardship about it. They were able to bifurcate their stewardship from the management aspect. That made them quite unusual."

Prior to the current board and management arrangement, the company operated with an executive management team consisting of family members and division managers who met monthly. Eventually, Roger and Tom developed a better structure to more clearly define everyone's roles. As it exists today, the original family printing business, EP Graphics, is a separate company owned by the family and its CEO, Tyler Kitt. While there are many ties, it remains a separate corporation with its own governance.

The publishing and fulfillment companies, the larger and faster growing part of the family's interests, are managed by CEO David McKee, who has been with the company since 1993. Tom and Roger spend time on DRG business, but aren't in the office every day. They're not on the golf course fulltime, either, although Roger, who played on his college golf team, would like to be. Instead, they oversee other family business interests including the Berne Tri-Weekly News, EP Graphics, a local furniture manufacturer, and various real estate ventures. They're also both very active in church and civic affairs.

A board 'with teeth'

The Muselmans say their board of directors is pivotal to the success of their family-owned, non-family managed company. "We decided that, to really make this work, Roger and I had to be accountable to someone," says Tom Muselman. "We wanted an outside board of directors with teeth." He and Roger are the only family members on the board, which includes four outside directors and CEO McKee.

The board isn't merely a ceremonial group that meets once a year to rubber-stamp management decisions. "The outside members of the board are chosen for their knowledge and experience in the businesses that we are in," McKee explains. "We have been blessed with some people on the board who have been very successful and have been eager to help us improve our business. They work not just in an advisory role on the board but have helped us with a certain amount of hands-on. They even help with some hiring and product decisions. It's a very healthy, collaborative working environment. At the same time, they're very careful not to step on our toes operationally."

The four outside board members are Paul Hale, an investment banker specializing in media; Tom Curl, former CEO of Reiman Publications in Greendale, Wis.; Jeanne Voigt, founder and president of catalog and online retailer MindWare; and John Ehlert, founder and chairman emeritus of Ehlert Publishing Group.

Voigt, who has served on DRG's board for two years, characterizes the board as more active than many others. "We have a very good, open discussion of issues as a total group," she says. "We're involved in all of the discussions about the business and how they should run it. We look at the strategic plans and have a lot of involvement in those issues." What's more, she adds, "When we're trying to recruit board members or employees, or considering acquisitions, the board is involved in that process. They'll use us as leverage to meet people and get things accomplished for them."

"The board isn't just our friends from the golf course, our attorney or accountants, our uncles and aunts," Roger points out. "They're active and competent." The board meets in person quarterly, confers by telephone in months when there is no full meeting, and works on projects on an as-needed basis in between. There are also board committees to handle compensation, incentive plans, and the stock appreciation plan that applies to the top three executives, as well as an audit committee and a human relations committee.

"The outside directors don't get into the family side," Tom explains. "They focus on helping us increase shareholder value." That means operating results, according to Tom: "This board of directors can be a pain in the rear. They're tough. They're just dollars and cents, black and white. They're animals when it comes to results." He's obviously happy with that.

Consultant Leslie Dashew, who worked closely with the Muselmans as they made the transition to family investors, says this type of board enables that kind of arrangement: "How do we make sure we have oversight that guarantees the business is being run properly? You need a good board of directors."

She recommends that outside directors not just have objectivity and expertise, but also have experience with some of the situations and developments the family is facing. If their goal is to double the size of the business, the board member should have done that someplace. If they are transitioning from family- to non-family management, they should have board members who participated in that process at some point in time.

What's next for the Muselman family and DRG? They recently came close to an acquisition that would have doubled the size of the company, according to Roger, but decided against it. The company's latest move is the acquisition of a concept from the Washington Post Company, Town Square, a magazine title tested but not rolled out by the previous owner. It will focus on the joys of small-town life, a step away from the core titles now offered by DRG. All content will be provided by the readers, a concept honed and polished by board member Tom Curl when he was president of Rieman Publications.

The oldest member of the fourth generation, Tom's daughter Shannon, is still in her teens, so some important decisions are still a few years in the future. In the meantime, Roger says, "We're really happy with what we're doing. We're having a good time and investing for the future. The goal is to keep it a family business."

Originally published in Family Business, www.familybusinessmagazine.com.

Chapter 39

Case Study: Mixing Family And Non-family Owners

"We try to be open, transparent, and

explain to everybody what's going on."

The roots of one of suburban New York's largest real estate firms run deep—all the way to County Kerry, Ireland. That's where the founder of what is today Houlihan-Parnes Realtors, Daniel Houlihan, immigrated from in 1874 at the ripe young age of 14. Young Dan started as a construction laborer but eventually created a real estate business that today owns or manages millions of square feet of commercial property across the country.

Jim Houlihan, 58, Dan's great-grandson, runs the firm today with a staff of 55 in the White Plains, NY, headquarters and more than a thousand others at various properties across the country. Houlihan joined the company in 1973, the same year it moved from the Bronx to Westchester County. "After my junior year in college, my father suggested I try working in his office for the summer," he explains. "Since I didn't have to be at work until nine, that sounded much better than the six AM start I had for a summer job working for a moving company in the Bronx the previous year." After college, he worked as a broker for the company for fourteen years before becoming a partner. His two daughters, Christy and Kelly, have both worked with the firm but are currently completing advanced degrees, Christy in law and Kelly a master's in real estate management. Houlihan doesn't know for sure if either or both will join the firm, but he wouldn't be surprised.

Houlihan-Parnes has survived and prospered for 120 years by being nimble. Around World War I, Dan's three sons joined the company and pioneered development of the Woodlawn and Wake-field sections of the Bronx. During the Great Depression, they managed and sold thousands of foreclosed properties, then stepped up during the recession of the early 1990s to buy over a billion dollars-worth of properties from the Resolution Trust Company and the FDIC. Major expansion began when Jim Houlihan became a partner in 1987 and acquired a number of affiliated real estate service companies, investment firms, and management companies.

As with many family businesses, there are both actively employed family members (two of Jim Houlihan's brothers, a brother-in-law, and a cousin) and numerous family members with investment interests in either the company or its various properties. "I've seen in other families where jealousy gets involved," Houlihan points out. "They get into crazy situations where the kids are suing their mother or one brother won't talk to another brother. Everybody's happy when things are going good, but when you go through a down-turn like we have in the last couple of years, you can have people pointing fingers and raising questions. We try to be open, transparent, and explain to everybody what's going on so you don't get spears thrown at your back." They have a family business council that meets annually. The company also sends out financial updates and other news throughout the year.

Even with its success in the U.S., the family has never forgotten its Irish immigrant roots. Jim Houlihan was awarded the Ellis Island Medal of Honor in 2000 and served as Chairman of the committee that created the Great Hunger Memorial unveiled in 2001 at V.E. Macy Park in Ardsley, NY. Later, he chaired the committee that raised funds for The Rising, the memorial dedicated to the 109 Westchester County residents who perished on September 11.

Chapter 40
Case Study: Adapting To A Changing Market
"He was adventurous and had an entrepreneurial spirit."

Manny Dubinsky did what his customers asked. That's how he went from repairing jacket zippers in the Bronx to selling giant umbrellas that shade diners at sidewalk cafes around the world at ZipJack Custom Umbrellas. Today, his daughter Martha continues the tradition of responding to customers as she fashions the company he left her into a business suited for the twenty-first century.

"My father always said it's not all about the all-mighty dollar," Martha Dubinsky says. "It's about building solid relationships. If you take care of people, everything else will take care of itself."

Her father started the company in the Bronx in 1950. He began fixing zippers on jackets (ergo the name "ZipJack") using a skill he learned in his parents' coat factory. "An army buddy taught him how to fix rain umbrellas," she explains. "Then someone asked one day if he knew how to re-cover a garden umbrella, so he said 'yes' even though he'd never done it before. My mother thought he was crazy. Later, someone asked him to put a logo on an umbrella, which he'd also never done. But he was adventurous and had an entrepreneurial spirit."

Manny's work caught the eye of beverage giants Perrier and Schwepps and the company took off. Today, ZipJack produces umbrellas for Cinzano, San Pellegrino, TGI Fridays, Chili's, Subway Restaurants, and many others. Country clubs and resorts are big customers, too. If you've ever dined in Rockefeller Center, at a Grand Hyatt or a Marriot Hotel, you've probably sat beneath one of ZipJack's products.

Martha, now 48, worked in the shop in her teens then joined the company full time after she graduated from SUNY Purchase with a degree in fine art. "My father believed you had to understand what you are selling from the ground up, so I started working in the back. Later, when I started in sales and operations, I knew more about what I was doing." Her older brother followed a different path and today chairs a university English department in South Carolina. Her husband, Michael Witkowski, works with her as operations manager.

Manny passed away in 2006. Before then, Martha effectively ran the company while both her father and mother dealt with the end stages of cancer. "He wasn't the kind of teacher who rammed it down your throat," she says, "but since he passed away, I still hear him talking to me."

Since Martha took over, she's refocused the business. Her father marketed heavily to specialty patio retailers who sold to consumers. Imports and big box stores undermined that market, so she concentrated the company's efforts on the custom commercial market. She explains, "I targeted customers like country clubs, restaurants, swim clubs, and others who need a higher quality, more durable product." Martha encourages the patio retailers who were formerly the company's main customers to reach out to the restaurants and other commercial accounts in their areas, essentially serving as dealers for ZipJack. "They're starting to make money doing that," she says.

"We're still sort of transitioning from my father's era to mine, but that's smoothing out," she says. Some things won't change, though. "I never want to get so big that I don't know people's names or recognize a face."

Chapter 41

Case Study: Family Dynamics Move The Business
"You never get a break because
you're always with your family."

Family dynamics take on added velocity when business is involved. At least that's the experience of Joe Pepe, President and COO of Pepe Auto Group in White Plains, NY. The six-dealership company works its way through family squabbles and parental control issues though, and uses family ownership to its advantage.

"We all get along together fine, but there are sibling rivalries," says Pepe, who works with his 80-year-old father and two of his three brothers. "Plus you never get a break because you're always with your family." His older brother, Sal, 57, runs the Larchmont store, and younger brother Bob, in his late forties, works with all the dealerships. Another brother opted out of the business and went into real estate.

Pepe's father, Gene, started the company in 1968 and family dynamics may have influenced that decision, too. "My father was working for his father in a construction and real estate business and didn't like it," Pepe explains. "He always had a fascination with cars, so he bought an Oldsmobile dealership in Mount Vernon. In 1970, he bought out his partner and picked up the Mercedes-Benz franchise." Today, Gene Pepe remains CEO and is very active in painting the bigger picture for the company. That also creates interesting family dynamics, according to Joe. "My father looks on us as kids, whereas we're adults," he says. "It's hard for him to let go and it can be a difficult situation."

On the other hand, interaction with family members has a positive side, too. "We all own these businesses together, so we make decisions based on what's best for the company, not what's best for an individual," Pepe says. "We talk together every day and that helps us make decisions that are right for everybody."

The company today has over 300 employees and operates six dealerships in suburban Westchester County, NY: Mercedes-Benz in White Plains and Larchmont, Porsche and Infinity in White Plains, Sprinter Commercial Vans in White Plains, and the newest addition, Cadillac in Yonkers. They've been notably successful, too. Pepe Infinity was the largest selling dealership of that nameplate in the country in 2010 while Mercedes Benz White Plains is in the top 20 in sales and the Larchmont store is number 32 in the nation out of about 600 dealerships.

Pepe believes family ownership is at least partially responsible for their success. "I can make a decision immediately," he says. "When you work for a big conglomerate, you can't get an answer right away. It's discouraging for employees." He adds, "It matters tremendously to our customers, too. If someone wants to meet the owner, I'm here every day."

Chapter 42

Case Study: The Family Tyrant

"Whenever you start up your own company,
you can tell people the way you want things done."

Ping Golf has revolutionized not just an industry but also a sport played by nearly 29 million Americans. The innovative product designs of company founder Karsten Solheim made a difficult game easier—and a lot more fun—for golfers at all levels. His sons, especially CEO John Solheim, 61, honed a business model that set standards for the industry. Today, the third generation is getting ready to assume the mantle of leadership while fourth-generation Solheims will be coming along soon. They are inheriting a $300 million operation with 1,000 employees, about 850 of whom work at the main campus in Phoenix, Ariz.

It all started with Karsten Solheim's obsession with the game, which he didn't take up until age 42 while still an engineer at General Electric. He began experimenting with clubs and patented his first product, a putter that on contact with a ball made the distinctive sound that gave the company its name, in 1959. Production took place in the garage and was literally a family affair. John Solheim was 13 at the time. "When we started, I drilled the holes in the putters where the shaft went," John recalls. "My brother Allan was putting the grips on. It was fun."

That first putter's heel and toe weighting helped the player keep it on line. It evolved into the Anser model, which featured several other advancements. "If you look at nearly every putter on the market today, they're all descended from the Ping Anser," says John Buczek, former head golf professional at the fabled Winged Foot Golf Club in Mamaroneck, NY, and PGA National Merchandiser of the Year for 2006. "It's amazing what they've done in the golfing world since Karsten developed the original Ping putter in his garage," Buczek says. "They've been leaders in putters, in irons, and even in golf bags."

The first major tournament win for the company came in 1969, when George Archer used an Anser Putter to win the Masters. Every time a tour player wins an event using a Ping putter, a gold one is inscribed and given to the player and a duplicate is placed in the company vault to commemorate the occasion; more than 2,300 of them are there today. Angel Cabrerra, the 2007 U.S. Open winner, uses Ping clubs, as does the world's leading female player, Lorena Ochoa, and Daniel Chopra, the winner of 2008's first PGA Tour event, the Mercedes Championship. The company sponsors the Solheim Cup, the premier international event for women pro golfers.

Karsten's way

As with any family business, Ping's path hasn't always been smooth. Karsten, who suffered from Parkinson's disease and died at age 88 in 2000, was a brilliant engineer, but his management style evokes mixed reviews from family members and longtime employees. "Karsten's Way," the name of a street on the company campus, also describes the man's strong grip on the corporation's direction. "Growing up, I was told there was the right way, the wrong way and Karsten's way," says John's youngest son, David, 28, who works in corporate communications. "Whenever you start up your own company, you can tell people the way you want things done. It's been a while since he was here, but that idea has not left the place."

"Part of the Karsten way is doing things right because it's the right thing to do, not necessarily the right business thing to do," says Stacey Solheim Pawels, Karsten's granddaughter and John's niece, who is vice president and corporate secretary.

Karsten's way brooked no opposition, whether from within the company, the family or the powers-that-be in the golf world. In 1961, he created another revolutionary product, the cavity-back iron. The initial primitive version became the Ping Eye2, a forgiving, game-enhancing club that, along with an innovative custom-fitting system, gave Ping a commanding 40% of the market for irons in the 1980s. The clubs also caused immense trouble for the company and the family. In 1988, the United States Golf Association ruled that the clubs didn't conform to the rules of the game. The next year, the PGA Tour announced they would ban the clubs, too. A long legal battle ensued.

That battle was a source of friction between John and his father. "The USGA thing really strained our relationship," John says. "I wanted to get it over with because it was draining him so much." Karsten also refused to introduce any new irons until the suit was settled. In 1990, the USGA settled by approving the old clubs while

Ping agreed to design changes for new ones. The PGA Tour suit wasn't resolved (with acceptance of the design) until four years later . While Ping litigated, the rest of the industry moved forward technologically, beating Ping to market with lucrative metal and titanium woods.

The relationship between the two men had always been somewhat problematic. Even when he was making clubs as a teenager, John writhed under his father's management. One early issue was money: "There was a shopping center that came into the area and I went there and applied for a job. It was only after that that I got paid [for working in the family business]," he recalls. "I got $2.50 a putter, but if I needed help to get the job done, I had to pay the employees out of my own pocket. I had some of my high school friends helping."

The real internal battles came when it was time for Karsten to step aside. "My dad didn't want to let go," John says. "He would never talk about not being there. That made the planning pretty difficult." It was even more difficult when Karsten became ill. "When the Parkinson's started to get to him, I realized I needed to step in," John explains. "I discussed it with him, but he didn't want to do that [step down] Finally, before a board meeting, I told him I wanted to nominate him for chairman, which we'd never had before, and he would nominate me for president. He had a few words in private with my mother, and that's the way it happened." John later learned that his father had made the decision to turn over voting control of the company stock to him some time earlier but kept it secret as he held on to the bitter end. His two older brothers were co-executive vice presidents until they retired.

Generational shifts

When John took over in 1995, the change supercharged the company. He expanded the product line into metal woods, set up a rapid-delivery system to hold on to the company's position in the custom-fitting market and hired Ping's first advertising agency. He also divested several other operations that weren't directly related to the company's roots as a club maker.

Not long after, his own sons moved into management positions in the company. "At our age, the third generation has a lot more influence than the second generation did at the same age," David observes. "That's a credit to the second generation for allowing us to get our hands dirty."

Andy, 31, is director of customer relations. Domestic and international customer service, credit and club fitting and repair all fall under his aegis. Like his brothers (and his father, for that matter), he's never worked anywhere else. He says he learned what it means to be a Solheim early in his career. "One time, I had just finished my master's degree and had helped do a video for a national sales meeting," Andy recalls. "I was just going to show up, watch the video then go back to the office, so I was wearing shorts and a casual shirt. My father gave me 'the look.' Fifteen minutes later, I had a suit on."

John's oldest son, known as John K., is 33 years old and the one who inherited his grandfather's engineering talent. He holds an MBA as well as a degree in mechanical engineering. As vice president of engineering, he says, he has tried to expand the design function beyond the one-man-one-idea operation it was under Karsten. He's hired several design engineers with backgrounds in the sport and has concentrated on speeding the time to market for new products. One of the company's biggest changes came with the purchase—at John K.'s urging—of a supercomputer, which shortened the wait time for design analysis from 15 hours to 15 minutes.

"The Cray Supercomputer was one of those times when my dad and I were on the same page," John K. says. There were plenty of other times when they weren't, including several disagreements over product design. In fact, their relationship bears some resemblance to the one between Karsten and John, according to John K.: "We may have to name another road 'John's Way.' He has his own way of doing things."

That may not bode well for the looming management transition from the second generation to the third, although John says he's working to ensure a smooth handover of operations. "My dad was well into his 80s when he finally turned it over, and I don't intend for that to happen," John says. "I'm not in any hurry to leave, but, at the same time, we have to have the best person for the job. The family members have to compete with everybody else." The family is working with consultants to help them address succession issues.

John K. is often considered the heir apparent. Yet, he says, "Talking to my dad, I don't get a lot of that. He hasn't anointed me. Both of my father's brothers retired at 65, but I'm not sure what the plan is for him." Andy says he'd like the CEO job, too. "I don't know what my dad's plans are," Andy says. "I look at the third generation, and most of us are pretty young."

Leslie Dashew, a family business advisor in Scottsdale, says it makes sense for a business leader to take a cautious approach to succession decisions. "When families are thinking through this process, it provides a great deal of security to employees," she says. "If you want to run the business well, you run it like a business. You find the best talent. That may or may not be a family member."

Doug Hawken, 58, Ping's non-family president and COO, says he's not privy to the succession planning but feels good about the prospects. "We have a good balance of family members and non-family members at leadership levels," he says. Hawken might be considered a prospect to succeed John, but the two men aren't that far apart in age. Hawken says he only wants one thing: "Whoever takes on that leadership role at this company has to have the same passion as Karsten had and John has. You don't just assign somebody that passion. They either have it or they don't."

John turned the company around, streamlined it and worked through many of the rough spots, but there is still plenty of work to be done. Golf in the U.S. isn't a growing sport, according to John and many industry sources, but the international market is just waiting to be tapped. As John K. points out, "In Japan, we don't even have 1% of the marketplace. And that's the second largest golf market in the world!"

In recent years, Ping opened new assembly facilities in both Japan and Europe as part of its strategy to take its rapid delivery system to the international market.

There is also some low-hanging fruit domestically, according to John K. "We've been a little slow to adjust to the market's move from green-grass [golf course pro shop] outlets to retail stores," he says. "They've really taken over the hard goods side of the business. We have great relationships with the golf course owners and operators, but, at the end of the day, the consumer isn't buying product there."

Doug Hawken watched the generational transition from the vantage point of a non-family insider and offers a positive outlook for the future: "Since John has taken control, we've returned to a good position within the marketplace," he says. "We've had four years of growth now, but he's willing to listen to the fact that we need to get our group together to go forward."

Originally published in Family Business, www.familybusinessmagazine.com.

Chapter 43

Case Study: Learning At The Founder's Knee
"My father taught me that a business either moves ahead
and grows, or you're dying"

Many of us have mentors, but next-generation family business owners have a special bond with theirs. "When I was five years old, I could either go play baseball or go to work with my father," says Strauss Paper Company CEO Stewart Strauss. "I chose to go to work with my father." Today, Stewart, 57, and his sister, Joyce Jonap, 59, operate the $50-million company according to the lessons they learned at their father's knee.

Their parents, Henry and Ruth Strauss, fled Germany before World War II. "Neither one spoke English," Stewart says, "and they didn't own anything but the shirts on their backs." They worked numerous jobs and learned the language, though, and in 1943 Henry started a janitorial supply business out of the back seat of his car. By 1954, it occupied a 5000 sq. ft. building in Elmsford, NY.

"My father taught me that a business either moves ahead and grows, or you're dying," Stewart says. He joined the company in 1976. His brother-in-law, Bob Jonap, 61, became part of it in 1979, and his sister, Joyce, Bob's wife, in 1983. The company moved to Port Chester, NY, and today operates from 90,000 sq. ft. of warehouse, retail, and office space selling everything related to cleaning and maintenance to office buildings, schools, hospitals, and others in a 75-mile radius.

Strauss learned other lessons from his father as well. "Growing up here, I worked in every different job," he says. "Driving a truck, accounting, answering the phones. My father shifted me around so it was a major advantage to learn the business from the bottom up."

"It wasn't just the knowledge of operations, it was also building relationships with the employees. One of our drivers has been here 42 years. When I was fourteen he taught me how to drive a truck. In the last couple of years, he taught both of my kids how to drive."

"Those relationships can have a down-side, too. When I first became president of the company, it took a little time for some employees to realize I'm the same person but in a different role. When I make a decision, they have to move ahead with it."

The family hasn't come to any hard and fast conclusions about what's ahead for the company. Both Stewart and Joyce have two children ranging in age from 20 to 29. None work there today although all did during summers and after school. "This year, we are going to discuss with them their interests in coming into the company on a full time basis," Strauss says. The company has a rule that children must have five years of outside experience before joining the business. "It gives them perspective and knowledge," he explains. "If they are in the right position in the right industries, they can bring a big bag of tools to us."

He hopes they will, since family ownerships of Strauss Paper means a lot to him. "If our parents were alive today, they would be astounded at what this business is. We're very proud of what the family has done."

Chapter 44

Case Study: Mixing Technology With Tradition
"Revel in the company's rich history,
but don't rest on its laurels."

What would Clarence Wallauer think of a coupon texted to a cell phone? When he founded the paint and home decorating retailer that bears his name in 1921, only about a third of all households had telephones at all—much less miniature instruments that send signals through the ether. Today's Wallauer's, though, uses every marketing tool available to spread the word about the ten stores run by Clarence's grandson, Robert Duncan, Jr., and great-granddaughter, Debbie Duncan.

The Duncans revel in the company's rich history, but don't rest on its laurels. From an interactive website, Facebook page, and Twitter presence to staff training via webinars, they do their best to keep their stores as fresh as the paint on their customer's living room walls. Because they run what is essentially a visual business, they also continually change in-store displays and merchandise mixes to showcase new trends and styles. It's all part of the continual evolution of Wallauer's, which has grown from a single store in White Plains, NY, to seven more in Westchester and two in Putnam County. The largest is the North White Plains store, which has an 11,000 sq. ft. showroom plus warehouse and office space for company headquarters. They sell everything from industrial coatings to custom bedding, although 70% of sales come from the original product—paint.

Debbie Duncan handles advertising and marketing for the stores, skills she learned from her father, who serves as president. "I'm a lifer," she says. "I started in high school putting wall paper books away. I have worked in all the stores at one time or another." Her sister worked for the company until she moved to Florida five years ago." Both were literally raised in the business—the family lived in an apartment over the White Plains store at one time. "One day when my sister and I were very young," she says, "our father took us to the store in Tarrytown. We found a roll of wallpaper leaning against a ladder, so we got a roller and got up into the shop window and pretended to be live mannequins. We turned a few heads."

While the Duncans are proud that Wallauer's is entirely family owned, Debbie says she has no illusions about what that means. "I'm not sure being family-owned really matters to the customer," she says, "but being in business ninety years should mean something to them."

Will the company remain in family hands for the next ninety years? Hard to say, of course, but Duncan points out, "My nephew is only six, but you never know. He can already lift a wall paper book and pick out colors, too!"

Chapter 45

Case Study: Family Tragedy Shapes Company Future

"Despite the shock of losing their parents,

three brothers and their sister pulled together

to mount a ten-year battle to save their company."

Family business founders are often risk-taking entrepreneurs, but few can match the life-or-death exploits of Ben Abruzzo, who established a highly successful recreation and real estate business while making headlines as a record-shattering balloonist whose adventures captured the imaginations of millions of people around the world. His exploits in both arenas may be legendary, but they've been surpassed—both literally and figuratively—by his sons, Louis, Benny, and Richard Abruzzo, owners of the innocuously-named Alvarado Realty Company in Albuquerque, New Mexico.

The Abruzzo brothers came into control of the company in the worst possible way when their parents, Ben and Pat, were killed in a plane crash that also took the lives of four close family friends. Louis, the oldest, was only 29 when the accident occurred. He had just become engaged to be married. Benny was 27, Richard only 21, and the youngest sibling, Mary Pat (now deceased), was but 19. Despite the shock of losing their parents, the four pulled together to mount a ten-year battle to save the company.

"We thought of it as a collective challenge," Benny says. "The word was 'we' need to survive this, not 'I' have to."

And survive they did. Today, the $30 million (annual sales) company is best-known as the operator of the Sandia Peak and Santa Fe Ski Areas, and the Sandia Peak Tram, the longest conveyance of its type in the world and a major attraction for New Mexico tourists. But the company's holdings also include nearly two-dozen widely varied properties, including office buildings, shopping centers, apartments and even a small utility company. Until recently, it was one of the largest residential real estate developers in New Mexico. A fortuitous decision—mostly lucky timing, according to President and CEO Louis Abruzzo—led them to sell the last swath of undeveloped residential property they owned a year before the market crashed.

Company roots

The company's roots were put down by New Mexican developer and ski enthusiast Robert Nordhaus, who founded Alvarado in 1951. Ben Abruzzo, who had been stationed at New Mexico's Kirtland Air Force base, went to work for him in 1955 and bought into the Sandia Peak Ski Area in 1959. The two men, both high-energy, high-vision individuals, turned a primitive one-tow-rope ski slope into a bustling outdoor recreation center with 30 ski runs. Along the way, they also developed residential Sandia Heights in the foothills outside Albuquerque, where today the utility company they started still serves some 2,400 homes on lots they sold over the years.

Perhaps their biggest accomplishment was the construction of one of Albuquerque's best-known tourist attractions, the Sandia Peak Tramway, which at 2.7 miles in length, is billed as the world's longest aerial passenger tram. When they ran out of money getting the project literally off the ground, the men raised about $2 million using stock offerings, loans, and lines of credit from very nervous bankers. The tram's second tower, located at 8,750 feet, was built using helicopters because there were no roads that high up on the mountain. The tram opened in 1966 and has taken more than nine million passengers on the fifteen-minute journey to the mountain peak where they get an 11,000 square-mile panoramic view of the Rio Grande Valley.

To Louis Abruzzo, who was ten years old when the tram opened, the project was just another expression of his father's and Nordhaus's vision and drive. "During the sixties and seventies, they were on fire," he says. "They were borrowing, and leveraging, and building, and expanding and somehow they managed to do it and make it through." While Nordhaus remained on the board of directors, eventually Ben Abruzzo acquired controlling interest in the company.

Seeking more challenges

Ben Abruzzo's ambitions extended beyond the entrepreneurial, however. In 1978, he won worldwide fame when he and two partners completed the first successful trans-Atlantic balloon flight in Double Eagle II, a helium balloon they flew for 137 hours. Just three years later, he was part of the team that made the first Pacific crossing in a balloon in Double Eagle V, sailing 5,768 miles from Japan to California.

"We were all a part of his ballooning activities as we were growing up," says 45-year-old Richard Abruzzo. "He was flying hang gliders off the top of the mountain and landing in the front yard." As often as not, his wife and children were with him.

"Growing up, we were all flying hang-gliders and stuff like that and never thought anything about it," Louis says. "If a cliff was there, jump off it. If something had wings, fly it. Balloons, hang-gliders, sail planes, jumping off the crow's nest of ships into the ocean—there just were no boundaries. We were coaxed along to try everything. I used to do drops from my dad's balloon on a hang-glider. He'd take me up to 12,000 feet, then cut me loose and I'd fly my hang-glider down and think nothing of it. I was in my 20s." He adds, "We grew up in a little different environment than most people. My Mom had to just grin and bear it."

All three sons are still outdoor enthusiasts, although not quite as active as they once were. Louis races bikes and still has a pilot's license, but says he doesn't use it much since he sold his aerobatic stunt plane three years ago. Benny's passion is heli-skiing and rock-climbing. Richard skied competitively in college and followed his father into the skies as a record-setting balloonist. In 1992, he and a partner broke his father's world record for the longest flight in a balloon (over six days in the air) when they were blown off course during a trans-Atlantic race and ended up in Morocco. In 2003, he made the first transcontinental solo balloon flight, which took him from California to Georgia. Just a few years ago, he nearly died after a balloon he was racing floated into thermal conditions that sent it into a power line in Kansas.

The tragedy

None of the boys' exploits matched the challenge they faced in February, 1985, though, when they suddenly found themselves in charge of a sprawling, high-profile business empire that had just closed on its largest (at the time) acquisition, the Santa Fe Ski Area. Ben Abruzzo was flying his wife, Pat, and four of her closest friends to Aspen for a ski vacation. Louis had just become engaged that Christmas, and he and his bride-to-be, Stacy, were picking out their wedding rings when he got the call telling him his father's plane had gone down. Benny was in Santa Fe, where he had moved to run the ski area they had acquired the previous October.

Richard and Mary Pat were in college and still living at home. Benny and his wife, Sandra, moved back into the family home with them to, as he put it, "provide them with a family environment for the first year or so while things settled and everybody got more grounded." Louis and Stacey went ahead with their wedding in June because he felt his parents would have wanted them to.

"Having lost both parents simultaneously took the level of difficulty to the maximum," Richard says. "But when you're faced with tough situations, you just figure it out."

In addition to the immense personal loss, there were very pressing business matters that required immediate attention. "We essentially had to go right back to work," Benny explains. The newly-acquired Santa Fe Ski Area required massive renovation of buildings, equipment, and the ski runs. Benny was running both ski areas before the tragedy. He says, "It was very difficult times. I just went to work every day, figuring that if I worked harder, it would help."

"There were a lot of good people involved in these companies and that helped tremendously," Richard points out. "They were very much a part of getting us through those times." Bob Murphy, a key executive in the company, oversaw the residential real estate developments.

The IRS challenge

Louis handled the commercial real estate and the tram, but also took on the largest task of all—dealing with the IRS and the estate. His father's estate planning had been rudimentary at best. "My father didn't put much value on all that," Louis explains. "He was much more concerned about building wealth through real estate using leverage and inflation. There was some life insurance, but it was inside the estate so it was taxed. With all his balloon adventures, we had talked about his death, of course, but it was always assumed he would be the one who went." No one anticipated the massive estate event that occurred when both parents died.

"That was really a difficult, grueling time," Louis says. "We had to borrow to pay taxes and it took a decade to settle that. The IRS assessment was two and a half times ours. We essentially liquidated our personal assets and used up everything else—homes, lots, cash, and all the income the companies earned during that period—in the ten years it took to save the family business. But at the end of the day, we preserved ownership in the company."

Difficulties with the IRS weren't the only ones the brothers faced during that decade. "We kind of got stuck in that savings and loan crisis where we had loans called and needed to be re-financed," Louis explained. "It stayed pretty challenging until 1995, when we emerged."

Just after the financial problems were settled and the brothers thought the worst had been put behind them, Mary Pat died. "That was very, very, very hard," Louis says. "We were just coming out of the financial problems. She had some heart and other health issues, but when she died at age 31 it was quite a shock." Mary Pat was working part time in the marketing department of the tram when she passed away.

Liquidation not an option

The easiest route through all these travails might have been to liquidate and move on, but none of the brothers says that was even considered. "Our Mom and Dad gave us such a great example," Benny says. "Their actions were such that walking away from something wasn't an option. Dad always persevered and Mom was always there to support him. While they were building the tram, he got into financial difficulties, but he saw it through. He even fell off the tram and was injured, but he survived that. The balloon in the ocean [Ben Abruzzo's first trans-Atlantic attempt ended in near-tragedy]....I could go on and on. The way we were raised as kids, you dusted yourself off and moved forward."

They may have played hard, but they worked hard, too. "Dad was quite a task master," Richard says. "There was always a long list of chores. That could be as crude as throwing rocks off a ski

271

trail to cleaning the bathrooms at the tramway to picking up cigarette butts off the top of the mountain."

"We grew up in an adventurous household," Louis adds, "but
if we went skiing on Sunday, we went to church on Saturday
night."

A few years ago, Louis says, they restructured the companies
by unwinding fifty years of corporate tangles. During that process,
they bought in several million dollars' worth of outside stock holdings, although there are still some 45 non-family shareholders.
Over 80% of the stock is now in the hands of family members.

While they are conscientious about preserving the business
their father left them, the brothers haven't rested on their laurels.
The ski areas and tram are solid performers and, while they are currently out of the residential real estate business, they now own
three office complexes, one in Phoenix, the other two in Albuquerque. They own and operate neighborhood retail centers between 50,000 and 100,000 square feet throughout New Mexico,
southern Colorado, and Texas. A recent report by Compass Bank
says Alavardo's book value has grown four-fold since Ben Abruzzo's death, accomplished while paying the shareholders about 40%
of its earnings in the form of dividends each year.

"Fortunately for us, by luck and design we've entered this new
economic era, which is not good or pleasant for anybody, but we're
well poised to get through it," Louis says. "We're looking for other
opportunities. We probably like to buy some more retail and office
properties."

Even with their eyes firmly on the future of their business, the Abruzzo brothers take time to indulge their passion for outdoor adventure. They're passing it along, too. In December, Benny put his grandson in a back pack and took him down a ski slope at the ripe old age of eight months.

Originally published in Family Business, www.familybusinessmagazine.com.

Chapter 46
It's Never Too Soon To Plan for Succession
"Key succession questions for you, your attorney, and your accountant."

When—not if—you no longer run your business for some reason, what will happen to it? How will that major development affect your lifestyle? Those are questions more and more company owners face as they contemplate retirement, unforeseen illness, or the many other twists and turns on the road to the future.

"We've been thinking about it," says Kerry Wilson, manager of Windrush Gallery in Fairfax, VA. She owns the gallery with her mother, Sylvia, and her sister, Candi. "It's been on our minds, but we haven't done anything about it." That pretty much sums up most small business owners' approach to the situation.

The simplest and easiest (sort of) solution is to sell the gallery to an outsider or just liquidate the assets and walk away when the time comes. Given the intensely personal nature of many businesses, however, selling to an outsider is no slam dunk and liquidation can yield a pittance when stacked against the financial demands of retirement. Long, detailed conversations with your attorney, accountant, and financial planner should begin literally years before you decide on either step.

Ellwood Jones, President of Capital Regional Financial Planning Group in Sacramento, CA, observes, "In my experience, small
businesses sell to inside people more often than they sell to outsiders." Those insiders can be family members, key employees, or
even customers with extremely strong ties to the company. Selling
to one of them isn't something to be undertaken lightly either, considering the consequences. "The business may be the biggest asset
they have," Jones says, which means its successful disposition can
have a huge impact on the business owner's lifestyle in retirement.

Show of Hands Gallery in Denver, CO, started as a coopera-
tive of sixteen artists in 1983. Debbie Kneale, co-owner, is the last
of the original members. "In essence, I've been through this fifteen
times," she says. "Our accountant wrote up an agreement that gives
the business first option to buy out—at book value—the shares of
the person who wants to leave. We really wanted to protect the
entity of the business."

"If the remaining partners couldn't or didn't want to exercise
the option, they still had the right to approve any outsider who
might buy the shares of the departing partner," Kneale explains.
"That way they couldn't sell their shares to their obnoxious
cousin." When it came time for her to buy out the last original
partner seven years ago, she didn't want to be the sole proprietor,
so those shares were sold instead to current partner Douglas Brugger. "We still operate under the same agreement," she says.

What happens next? Kneale is 54, partner Brugger is 43, and
they're actively thinking about that question now. Neither partner
has family to take over the gallery and they recognize that selling to

employees is far from an ideal solution. "Those folks may not have the capital, so there is the question of whether you want to remain tied to the lease, carry a note, and so on," Kneale points out.

Attorney Roger Hurwitz, partner in Slagle, Bernard & Gorman in Kansas City, Missouri, is a Fellow of the American College of Trust and Estate Counsel and has practiced law in this area for fifty years. He says, "The first issue is the competence of the successor, whether it's a child, a friend, or whatever. Is that person competent to manage the business?" Company owners may hope to teach their successor the ins and outs of their business, but that takes time, too. "Business owners are not good teachers," in Hurwitz's experience. "It takes effort to teach. The successor can learn a lot by watching, but it takes a lot of active teaching, too."

Kneale agrees. "Unless they intend to employ you to do some extensive training, go to the shows with them, and help with the buying, it could be difficult to just hand them the keys and walk away," she says.

Looming over the entire situation, of course, are the financial implications of transferring the business to another owner, regardless of whether that person is your offspring, a partner, a key employee, or a complete stranger. "When it comes to taxes and inheritance, I don't want to be penalized," Wilson says succinctly.

"What's the annual after-tax income they want in retirement?" Jones says. "Everything flows from that number. They also need to know what the current value of their business is. If the value is large enough, they can sell it and retire. Quite candidly, most owners have no idea what they need for retirement or what the value of their business is."

Here are some key succession questions for you, your attorney, and your accountant:

- Do you expect the new owner to be an insider or an outsider?

- When will the transfer take place?

- How will the price be determined?

- How will the purchase be financed?

- How much training will the new owner need?

- How will management retain key employees? Artists?

- Will a sale impact your financial future?

- Can you maximize gallery-supported retirement funds?

- How can income and transfer taxes best be minimized?

Again, the sooner you start planning for succession, the better off you will be. "You can't start planning too early," Jones adds. "Once you've survived the five-year startup period, you need to start looking at your ultimate goals. If we can get at least a ten year run, that's good. You can budget it in, and if you have a bad year you can make it up, all of those things. Three to four years is minimum."

Jones poses other questions that can be answered and problems that can be addressed if there is enough advance planning: Is the cash flow large enough to support a buyout while leaving the buyer enough to live on until it's completed? Are there key managers who need to be retained and/or trained? Is there a business

277

plan that needs to be updated? Lease to be negotiated? Relation-ships between artists and the prospective owner that need to be developed?

It may seem like something you can always deal with later, but succession planning is best done far in advance for a number of reasons. Prime among them is your own financial security and peace of mind, but your partners, employees, customers, and artists all have a stake in your decisions as well. So does your Uncle Sam and several other interested tax collectors. Scarlett O'Hara's im-mortal words, "I'll think about that tomorrow" should have no place in your vocabulary.

Section Six
Wit & Wisdom

The only thing better than learning from your own mistakes is learning from the mistakes of others. In this section, dozens of small business owners and managers share their experiences with customers, employees, competitors, vendors, and even government regulators. They also brainstorm about ways to improve their companies. Their stories will help you become a better manager.

What would make your business more successful? I asked retailers, manufacturers, restaurant owners, service providers, and many others what they needed to take their companies to the next level. I also asked them to share the lessons they've learned over the years with other business operators. Sharing their thoughts and experiences are managers of convenience stores, health clubs, sporting goods retailers, LP gas distributors, automotive service providers, golf course operators, and restaurateurs. Their stories are wistful and whimsical as well as insightful and practical.

Chapter 47
Invent This...Please
"Creative ideas for inventions that could impact
the way we work and run our companies.

The electric light bulb transformed civilization. For better or for worse, so did the cell phone that takes pictures. More than a few business owners have a Thomas Edison side, too, as expressed in their creative ideas for inventions that could impact the way we work and run our companies.

Joe Stone is CEO of Systems & Methods Inc., in Carrolton, Georgia, a company founded in their living room by his father in 1971, and which today does data-processing for governmental offices in several states. "We currently have some of the third generation that is starting to work in the company," Joe says. "We have everything from in-laws to outlaws to ex-laws."

His father, Bob, turned over day-to-day operations in a well-planned succession, but Joe likes the idea of having him available for frequent consultation. "I'd like to have a talking portrait of him on the wall," he says. "He's the founder, and a lot of our company culture is built around what he stood for and what he still stands for."

When it comes to the next generation, Joe says he'd like to leave them a time capsule: "It would have something my father always said to me in it: keep an open mind and a broad sense of humor. You've got to approach every day just like that."

Chris Combe, President and CEO of Combe Incorporated in White Plains, New York, likes the idea of another kind of capsule. "I love the energy and fun of creative meetings," he says. "How about a capsule that keeps innovation at top of mind 24/7?" Chris' company was founded on the innovative personal care ideas of his father, Ivan. Today it produces products like Just For Men Hair-color and Johnson's Foot Soap. In addition, Chris says, "Please invent the genie that will grant each of our world-wide employees passion for his or her work every day!"

L.R. Gardner, who works for his father running their chain of 22 Cracker Box Convenience Stores in Arkansas, would appreciate a real-time father-son communications device. "He promoted me once and I didn't know about it until I got new business cards," he relates cheerfully. "They said I was vice president. I wondered if that would show up on my paycheck, but it didn't. At least I got new business cards."

Having a management position in the family business means multi-tasking, according to L.R., which would make a dial-up data-base of how-to instruction good to have. "I found out I'm the IT director here, too," he says. "How did I find that out? If something breaks and everybody screams at you to come fix it, you're the IT director. I've got about seventeen hats and one salary."

Speaking of salary, L.R. says, "If my father were talking about my salary, he'd point out how much extra money I get every month. He'd have some illustrations and maybe a pie chart." He figures his father doesn't need any inventions to explain it any more clearly than that.

Chapter 48
Industry Insights: Convenience Stores
"Attach a monofilament line to every dollar bill that comes into the store so we could retrieve it at the end of the day."

Something that would tame government interference tops the industry invention wish list of many people, including L.R. Gardner. He says, "You got the government collecting taxes. You've got the government interfering in worker's comp; you've got OSHA; you've got the environmental people. It's an unending, never ceasing line of government people that have nothing better to do. It is an affliction—a virus."

"We need a spray for that," Gardner observes. "You can use pepper spray on them, but they don't take kindly to that. They have a tendency to come back with various and sundry armed personnel. And they'd probably get OSHA involved to tell you that you were using the pepper spray wrong. They'd want to know if you were wearing a protective mask while you were dispensing the hazardous chemical."

Stan Mills, President of Mills Squeegee Fill Stations in Lincoln, Nebraska, would like to see an invention to help him cope with another type of governmental regulation, sales-to-minors stings. "It would be nice to recognize the officers when they come on site with someone that looks like he's thirty-five years old when he's only eighteen," Mills says. "If we could somehow have an age detector that made them realistic. We had a kid down the street that had a beard like I'll never have—and he was in junior high school. He looked like mountain man when he was seventeen."

Cigarette snuffer

Yet another aspect of government's impact on the convenience store industry is taxes, especially cigarette taxes. When this issue was raised, Allan Foote said, "You really want me to comment on taxes? I thought this was a family publication!" Foote is the Director of Retail Operations for Blueox Corp., which operates ten Nice N Easy Grocery Shoppe stores in upstate New York. He'd like to see a cigarette tax equalizer that produced the intended result.

"What they're trying to do is get the message out there that cigarette smoking is not a good thing," Foote points out. "I just don't know if the way they're taxing them is the right way. When they raise taxes, I don't know how many people actually quit. Our business goes down, but how much of the business is going to the Internet and how much is going to the stores on the Native American reservations?"

Jimmy Morgan, President of J.R. Morgan Oil Co. in Carrollton, Georgia, would like to see a magic wand that solves the cigarette dilemma. As Morgan says, "I hate cigarettes and I'd love to do away with them, just as soon as they tell me something to replace the revenue with. The government is the same way."

Morgan points to another invention no one is likely to see soon, a price sign that tells the real story about gasoline prices:

"We're the only industry in the United States that has to post its price with tax included. I'd like to put my price on the street with 'plus tax' on the bottom of it."

Shrink wrap-up

Ideas for inventions that would deter, detect, or destroy thieves—both on and off the payroll—were plentiful among the retailers we interviewed.

"I don't know if you could attached a monofilament line to every dollar bill that came into the store so we could retrieve it at the end of the day," says Mills, "but that would be something to see."

"Drive-offs are another thing," he continues. "We need an inflatable state patrol helicopter that could be mounted on the canopy and slide over the edge onto the car in the event of a drive-off occurrence."

Morgan's thoughts on drive-offs were a little more aggressive. "I like the tire cutter idea," he says. "Like at the rental car company where, if you go out the wrong way, it'll cut your tires. If we put those in the driveway and the clerk got robbed or there was a drive-off, she could push a button and the tire cutters would pop up in the driveway and slash their tires."

Morgan also had an idea for a doorframe to handle both shrinkage and shoplifting. "Any product that goes out that door with a UPC code on it that has not been rung up, gets rung up on a little meter on the door. That way, if your employees are toting the product out of the store, or your customers are pulling it out of the store, your door has a little tally on it that tells you what's walked out the door that hasn't been rung up on the register." After considering it a moment, he refined his idea by adding a computer chip to be implanted in every human so that the sensor could just automatically charge their account for the merchandise. Sort of like a built-in debit card.

Employee motivator

Mills suggested that implanted chips could be useful elsewhere in retail store operations, namely, inside the employees' heads. "If employees had an internal time piece, that would be a good deal," he says. "We could implant a little chip in their head that would wake them up on time, let them know where their shoes, their uniform, and their name tags are, so when they left for work they'd be pretty much assembled without really thinking about it."

"I don't have much problem with people not making it to work on time," says Foote. "It's actually when they get there that the problems start. A lot of it is like babysitting. You have to guide them and encourage them to do things on their own and stuff like that." He goes on to point out that attitude is important, saying, "It would be nice if they could invent something would make the employees at least pretend to be happy."

Gardner says, "When we hire an employee, sometimes the biggest criteria is 'are they breathing?' and 'will they put the money in the drawer?' Sometimes, we're pretty liberal on the breathing part."

He wrapped up many of the invention ideas into one machine. "Invent a robotic clerk with some of that government-repelling spray. I'd like to have the patent on that," Gardner says, adding, "You need one with an extra arm for the mop to go on."

Privacy, please

Jimmy Morgan, President of J.R. Morgan Oil Co., needs a special invention to help control traffic in and out of his office because, well, sometimes a man just needs a little privacy.

"I tell everybody that, if I'm looking out the window while I'm on the phone, that means I don't want them in my office," Morgan says. "But they don't pay any attention. They come in anyway and just stand there, trying to get my attention." That's one problem. But the other is, perhaps, more serious.

Morgan has a restroom next to his office, and he used to have a red light outside the office rigged up to the light in the restroom so that employees would know where he was if they came looking for him. "You hate to announce to everyone that you're going to the restroom," he says. "Or they send someone back to your office and you step out of your restroom and there's someone setting there." Which is just another good reason to wash your hands when you're finished. But the red light was not a great invention, Morgan says: "I had to do away with it because it became known as the s'"'t light. It was the source of too many jokes."

Chapter 49

Industry Insights: Health Clubs

"An energy drink that tastes like beer

would be a perfect invention."

The health club industry is full of interesting people whose brain power matches their brawn. I asked several of them what inventions they'd like to see.

"The auto-flush toilet has already been invented," replied Mike Combes, "so it would have to be something else. We just got them, though, and what a difference it makes." Combes is General Manager of the Michigan Athletic Club in East Lansing and Genesys Athletic Club in Grand Blanc, Michigan.

Member happifier

Clean toilets is sort of a customer satisfaction issue, and Combes would like to see some other inventions that help in that area. "It would be great if someone could invent a pill or a drug that made the members happy with everything you did," he said. "Ninety-five percent of the people are great, but you end up with five percent that, no matter what you do, they're going to whine or cry or complain."

Since mandatory Prozac for all members isn't really practical, Combes had another idea that might accomplish the same goal: "We could use something that works like an airport metal detector that the members have to walk through. If they're not happy that day, they couldn't get in," he suggested. Having a machine like that would also mean, of course, that you wouldn't need to check the member's shoes for explosives, since they wouldn't be angry about anything.

Industry image enhancer

Several fitness industry pros asked for an invention to change the industry's image. As James Cummaro, owner of the Ardsley (NY) Athletic Club put it, "The reason this industry's only got 12 to 15 percent market penetration is because we're doing the same things we've been doing for thirty or forty or fifty years." Cummaro thinks lifestyle enhancement training is the answer and he'd like to see some technology applied to marketing it. He said, "Just because somebody can bench press 300 pounds doesn't mean they can move a couch around in their living room."

"Visuals are important," Cummaro said. So maybe we could enlist a Hollywood special effects wizard to invent a machine that melds video of a member working out with scenes of them leading their lives outside the gym. "We're turning the club membership into a lifestyle enhancement thing where they can take groceries out of the SUV," according to Cummaro. "They can shovel their snow better. They can chase their kids around. Their tennis game improves. That makes them feel better about themselves."

Speaking of visuals, Cummaro cites a major industry image factor that he believes keeps a huge number of potential members away. "One of the things that has hampered this industry is that people have this preconceived thing about what it's like to walk into a health club," he said. "They think everybody's beautiful and in incredible shape, but what about the 95% of the market that isn't? Everybody's not a supermodel or Arnold Schwarzenegger."

Mike Grondahl agreed with Cummaro. Grondahl is the owner of Planet Fitness, operator of five clubs on the east coast and franchiser of seven others. He said, "When it comes to marketing, the industry is pitiful, actually. It's way too intimidating."

"The fitness industry is run by aerobic queens, body builders, and people that are real hard core. That's a problem in this industry," Grondahl said. Perhaps someone should investigate genetic engineering to create a different breed of club owner, although Grondahl would like to see some mental constraints installed as well. "If I could invent one thing," he said, "it would be something that makes all the other owners understand that service is saying hello, saying goodbye, and keeping the place clean." There's that auto-flush toilet thing again.

Remote control employee

After members and owners, there's a third element in the club industry that certainly affects successful operations: employees. Some people would like to have a greater degree of control over who does what and how much of it they do.

"Forget personal training," Grondahl says. "Forget aerobic classes and spinning classes. How do you keep control over the service your member gets when you've got somebody that works for you only two or three hours a week?"

"Our philosophy is that we've got a manager that we pay well. Beyond that, it's more of an entry-level position so the door turns fast." Grondahl said. "Reducing turnover would be a help, but it wouldn't be worth the price." The thought of standardized, interchangeable front-line employees appeals to some in the industry, although no one came right out and suggested disposable trainers.

Combes, who oversees about 500 employees at the two clubs he manages, would also like to see some attention to employee capabilities. "Dealing with employees is one of the largest problems we face. Trying to get that many part time employees to do everything that we need them to do is one of our toughest challenges," he said, then he offered a solution: "A robotic front-line employee would be perfect. We don't pay a whole lot of money for someone to work the front desk, so they turn over a lot. They'd have to be a robot with a personality, though, like Rosie on the Jetsons."

Why does an employee have to have a personality? Because you need that particular feature to make the members happy, at least according to most marketing gurus.

Cummaro believes in hiring employees with personality and works to invent a sense of community at his club. "It's fun," he said. "We have parties. We do wine-tasting. We do bagels and lox on Friday mornings. There's a sense of friendship here. We've developed a place where people can come and sit and have an espresso, chat, and feel good about the other people that they're with."

The mention of food service gave Combes another idea for an invention that might be the most promising of all: "An energy drink that tastes like beer would be a perfect invention," he said. The members would like the taste, while at the same time they'd be drinking something healthy." And now that the auto-flush toilet has been invented, the fitness world is ready for it.

Chapter 50
Industry Insights: Sporting Goods Retailers
"A motivation mini-computer implanted in every employee."

Sporting goods retailers have a Thomas Edison side, too, as expressed in their creative ideas for inventions that could overcome some of the obstacles they face every day and impact the way stores are run and marketed in the future.

The single most requested item on the store operator's wish-list is a customer-expectations monitor, a machine that would let the staff know what the customer expects and then makes sure the service provided exceeds those expectations. As Steve Harding, President of Kep Harding's Sports Shops in Lincoln, Nebraska, says, "It's kind of a what-have-you-done-for-me-lately society. You can service them good for two or three years and deliver everything on time, but if you make one mistake or have a problem, they'll go down the street." He goes on to observe, "The loyalty isn't there like it used to be."

Schuylkill Valley Sports President Jerry Williams agrees, saying, "The biggest difficulty is just always maintaining customer service and focus. Every business talks about customer service but it's being prepared every day and having the right attitude. It starts not just in the stores but in the office and the warehouse. Our big thing now is exceeding the expectations of our customers. It's one thing to say but it's another thing to live it every day."

"The consumer's expectations continue to rise," adds Jeff Phillips, General Manager of running store franchiser Fleet Feet in Carrboro, North Carolina. "The expectation of service, the expectation that you'll have product in their size, the expectation that you'll have different ways they can shop with you." Phillips goes on to say, "There's plenty of product out there and there are plenty of outlets, particularly for running products, so the consumer can find what they're looking for in a lot of places. We have to provide an exceptional level of service if we expect to develop loyalty from our customers."

Motivation machinery

How do you exceed those expectations? A motivation minicomputer implanted in every employee might be one answer. "It really comes about if you have a willingness in the employee, then you can really train them to achieve those goals," according to Bruce Johnson, President of Gazelle Sports in Kalamazoo, Michigan.

Harding agrees that it starts with a motivated employee but, he says, "It's a little harder to find good ones. You really have to cater and have some decent benefits and make it a good working environment in order to keep good qualified employees."

Training ranks high on the list of almost every retailer we interviewed. Williams says he'd like someone to invent a customer service training program that's specific to the sporting goods retail industry. There are plenty of generic tapes and CD's on the market, but he's shopping for something that's going to apply to the unique selling environment like those in his company's fourteen stores in the Philadelphia area.

Johnson says specialty stores like Gazelle need an invention to help the staffer learn more about the customer, too. "The more information you can find out about them, the more you can help them," he points out. "But how does the customer know what they don't know? You can't problem-solve with them unless you're able to teach them and educate them about things that they don't know about."

Mature market merchandise

Inventions to better serve an aging sporting goods consumer are desperately needed, according to many of the retailers we questioned. "Where we've seen growth is in women and middle-aged and older folks getting into fitness programs for the first time," says Phillips. "They're looking for someone who can help them. They don't know much about running shoes or technical apparel, and there are not many places you can get that information."

"We're seeing a lot of older team leagues," agrees Harding. "Older baseball teams, adult soccer, adult this and that. We've even got an adult sand volleyball league in Lincoln. The fitness industry is addressing them with a lot more affordable treadmills and ellipticals and that kind of stuff and I think the sporting goods industry has to address the older athlete, too." Harding mentions another advantage of marketing to that group: "Sometimes, older people will spend a bit more money on an item, too. I know in golf, if somebody thinks it's a better club, they'll pay whatever it is. Same way in softball bats. We've seen the advent of some real expensive slow-pitch softball bats and it's usually the people in the older age groups that have the discretionary income to purchase that stuff."

A different, non-traditional kind of staffer is another way to better serve the mature market, according to Phillips. "We encourage our owners to try to hire staff that reflects their customer base," he says. "You can't have all skinny eighteen-year-old male employees who look like they just came from track practice. You need that forty-five-year-old woman who has been a full-time mom for ten years and whose kids are in school and is looking for some hours."

Johnson goes a step further, asking for someone to invent merchandise to meet the needs of another big, big market. "The population that is not thin" is not being served, he says. "Sixty percent of our population is obese. A lot of the apparel in our industry right now doesn't fit them. They want something to work out in. We sell shoes to people who maybe aren't athletic but need the footwear. There's a huge market out there for just providing their footwear."

Whiz-bang technology

Merchandise mix and the information technology that can help a store operator maximize return on inventory would be considered a blessing by many. As Johnson asks, "How accurate is that information that you're getting? In terms of return on investment, you can look at your financial statements by department and say that this department is better than the other department, but then you have to know more specific sorts of things. Is the technology out there to do that?"

"Our biggest problem is vendors delivering on time and making promises they can't keep," Harding offers. That could be an information technology problem, too. "You'll call or you'll fax in an order and the sizing mistakes, lettering mistakes, there are just too many mistakes in the pipeline. It seems to me that there is a tremendous amount of mistakes made that shouldn't be made."

Phillips believes there is large room for improvement in point of sale technology as well. He says, "Our industry has lagged behind. All our stores are implementing a new point of sales system that gives us a good ability to capture more consumer data." Fleet Feet's franchisees uses information like customer email addresses to send out periodic newsletters to build a community of runners loyal to the store.

Among all the inventions mentioned, one stands at the very top of everyone's list. It's a clock that gives you twenty-five hours in every day. As Johnson says, "If you're a business owner, you have the work you're trying to do and you have your family. Trying to balance those two is always a challenge. When you're at one, you feel like you should be at the other."

Chapter 51

If I Knew Then What I Know Now...

"Find a market niche and serve it well."

A pretty smart guy once said that you should learn from the mistakes of others because you can never live long enough to make them all yourself. That's never truer than in a small business, where every customer has a different problem that he expects you to solve and thin margins magnify even the smallest mistake. Fortunately, several successful business owners gave us a chance to learn some of the lessons they learned the hard way.

You don't get many mulligans in the sporting goods business, which is why Paul Drake says, "Don't rest on your laurels or the way you've always done things. Be prepared to change with the times." Drake, President of Fitness Pro in Savannah, GA, has witnessed plenty of change—and changed many times himself--since he went into business in 1977.

So have other long-time sporting goods retailers like Fred Baum, Baum's Sporting Goods in Tucson, AZ, and Randy Nill, Nill Brothers Sporting Goods in Kansas City, KS. All three say there weren't many things they'd do differently if they had the chance, but plenty they wish they'd done sooner. One of those things was to find a market niche and serve it well.

Niche marketing

Fifteen years ago, for example, Nill Brothers operated six full-line retail stores, offering warm-ups, running shoes, and other consumer lines along with equipment and uniforms. Today, they concentrate on the middle- to high-end team sports niche in four stores, leaving the rest of the market to the big box competition. What makes that narrow approach successful, according to Randy Nill, is total dedication to customer service. "We aren't the low price in town, especially on the school side," Nill says, "But we guarantee that, if you call before two, we ship your item out that day. For most of the schools in our area, that means one day service, even if the outside rep can't hand deliver it. They don't have to wait for the rep to come back into the office and return their call." Nill has been with the family company since his teens and worked there on a full-time basis since 1978.

Fred Baum's four Arizona stores are ultra-niche 100% baseball/softball operations, with half the business coming from Little League and the rest from schools. Most of his sales are paid for with booster funds and contributions, not through competitive bidding. Baum tells a story about why they changed: "I had a coach come in recently who was damn near in tears. He had put his hats out to bid and a local fly-by-night had bid the hats low and they are terrible quality. But the school district won't let him do anything about it because that was the low bidder."

"When we first started business, we were a pretty big bidding type operation, too" Baum continues. "But it's slow pay with terrible margins. Everybody and their brother bids against you." Today, he says, "The way we do business is much more relationship, much more quality of service, much more quality of product."

That's not to say that low price points don't have a place in the specialty store merchandise mix. Drake's three stores sell fitness equipment to both the commercial and the retail market and he's changed his philosophy about offering price points for all parts of the market. "For the longest time, we positioned ourselves as being kind of a boutique covering only the higher end products and not having the wide range that we have now," Drake says. "To have a $600 treadmill on the floor has been a big change for us. It's not that we sell that many $600 treadmills, but now we can capture that person in the store that originally didn't think they wanted to spend more. Now, we show them the $600 treadmill and the $2,000 treadmill and explain the difference. It keeps them from immediately walking out the door." This major shift enables Fitness Pro to "use that lower third of the prices to sell the other two-thirds of the stuff that we make our profits on," according to Drake.

Vendor friends or foes

Relationships with vendors provide plenty of fodder for "If I knew then..." speculation by these store operators. "Looking back, I wouldn't have been as committed to any one manufacturer as I was," Drake says. "We're their customer and sometimes they lose sight of that. They try to bully you around and strong-arm you." Drake reports that he recently stopped doing business with one big manufacturer all together. "It was a total restructuring of our business that cost us some money, but it taught me not to put all my eggs in one basket," he says.

Baum takes the opposite approach. "If I have a manufacturer that's taking care of us, I'll take care of them," he says. "A couple of years ago, we went to our top five or six suppliers and told them they have open PO's in our store. If they have a product that they think should be in our store, they can write it on the PO and send it to us. That trust in the relationship is unique."

Technology creeps in

When it comes to technology, many retailers wish they'd made a stronger commitment to online marketing. Nill explains some common thinking: " I had it in my mind for quite a while that, in our particular business, people like to come in and try out product—swing a bat, put a hand in a glove. So, for some years, I fought using the internet." What he found, however, was that the public was a few steps ahead. "People would come into our stores, try out about twenty gloves, and we'd hear the kid say 'Dad, I want this one' and we'd think we'd just sold a nice ball glove. Then Dad would say 'thanks a lot' and they'd walk out. Obviously, they were going to buy it on the internet."

Nill Brothers is on the web, but their site isn't equipped for e-commerce—yet. "We'll probably have capabilities for coaches to get online and place orders," Nill says. "Right now, we're still doing it with eight road guys calling on schools. That's still what we do and what we do best."

These operators may have 20/20 hindsight like the rest of us, but they have few regrets. When asked what else he'd do differently if he had the chance, Drake says, with a chuckle, "I can think of a whole bunch of stuff personally, considering I started running my own store when I was a 22-year-old bachelor living on Hilton Head. My store probably would have been a lot more successful sooner if I had paid more attention to business."

Chapter 52
Industry Insights: LP Gas Distributors
"Growth. It's wonderful to have, but it can be costly."

The LP Gas business is one where dealers and distributors have plenty of opportunities to err while they master the art of personnel management, the science of equipment maintenance, and the mysteries of financial accountability and where mother nature can lay on a mild winter that magnifies even the smallest mistake.

One of the big pitfalls in the propane business is growth. It's wonderful to have, but it can be costly, as Todd Hunsucker can attest. Hunsucker bought what is now Alliance Propane in Waldron, AR, from All Star Gas in 2005. "From the day we owned the business, we've made a ton of mistakes," he says honestly. "For one thing, I thought I needed every customer that walked through the door. If they wanted propane, I wanted to set a tank. Here I am, two years later, wondering what I'm going to do about the minimum usage customer. In ten years, the tank's not even going to pay for itself. But that's the one I thought I had to have."

Bryan Milton, who started Comstock Propane, Sparks, NV, in 2004 but had been a manager for AmeriGas for 25 years before, agrees with Hunsucker on the perils of jumping to set a tank for every possible customer. "I've got plenty of new opportunities coming in every day," He says, "but you have to be selective. I interview every customer, give them a written estimates, then take my time." He's interested not only in the return on his investment from the customer, but also whether they're going to be a good fit. "If somebody says they need it right now, there's usually an issue with the existing gas company. I give it a couple of days to see if they're the kind of customer I want."

You can also be a little too stringent when it comes to customer selection, according to Hunsucker. Troubled by unprofitable customers, he went to great pains to explain to his staff that they had to screen prospects a little better. "I told the secretary that we just couldn't afford to set a $500 tank for a customer with a space heater. It just wouldn't pay. But this gentleman came in who had built a huge shop for his lumber business. He called those heaters hanging from the ceiling in his shop 'space heaters,' so the secretary very politely told him we couldn't supply him. He was nice enough about it, but asked her for our competitor's telephone number." It was a potentially massive mistake, according to Hunsucker. But all turned out well in the end: "Thank goodness, a hand-shake and an apology on my part got the account after he'd bought only one tank of gas from my competitor."

People make mistakes

Among the many variables you have to juggle very day, perhaps none is so complex as the people you manage. Who do you hire? How do you get them to come to work every day? And persuade them to actually work while they're there? These questions are only the tip of the iceberg when it comes to employee matters, according to Mark Callahan, the third generation to run Callahan's

Gas in Centreville, MD. Callahan says, "I could write a book about hiring people."

"I decided one time to hire the least knowledgeable person who came in so I could teach him and shape him and mold him," Callahan relates with a rueful chuckle. "The smartest thing I did was make him sign an agreement that said he would owe me for his training class if he left within a year. The day he was supposed to go to class was the day he didn't show up again." Fortunately for Callahan, that day came only three weeks after the man started. "But three weeks was painful enough. I learned that lesson and moved on."

Charles Bell, who has owned Bell Oil & Propane in Van Buren, MO, since 1973, wasn't quite so lucky: "I hired a driver who was so bad I had to figure out his loads every day; how to load, what to drop here and there every day. After about a month or two, you should know where you're going and what you're supposed to do." Bell put up with the man way too long, a mistake he readily admits. "If somebody works for you for a full year and doesn't know any more than when he started, he's not good for your business," he says. "This guy could just never learn. He didn't apply himself, either."

Personnel problems are compounded when you're dealing with family members. Against his better judgment, Callahan once hired his younger brother. "He was too young," Callahan says. "I told him to take a year off after college—go have fun, go to Europe, go to the mountains and be a ski bum, but don't come here to work. Having said that, I told him I'd hire him if he wanted."

Which he did. But there were still wild oats to be sown and today, Callahan explains, "He's in Dallas having fun. I told him I'd take him back but it wouldn't be until after two years."

Equipment only stretches so far

Few operators make mistakes when it comes to buying new equipment—mainly because it happens so seldom that weeks of research and comparison shopping go into the decision. Even if something isn't quite right, as Bell says, "We just make it work some way."

Most dealers and distributors are like Callahan, who explains, "I research things way too much and make decisions way too slow, so I don't make many mistakes when it comes to equipment." A common mistake, though, is trying to get another thousand miles out of a truck that should have been sent to the bobtail graveyard a long time ago. "On the flip side, I keep things way too long and fix them way too many times," Callahan says. "I've kept a bobtail running that I wish I hadn't. I replaced the engine to keep it running, then compounded the mistake by getting it hydro-tested, so I was in it for another five years. Then the replacement engine caught fire, so I had to replace it again." Today? He points out, "It's been a great back up truck ever since."

Pushing vehicles past their prime is a temptation just about any kind of business can face, but one of the unique equipment problems LP dealers have is the array of conflicting state and local regulations just waiting to snag you up. Hunsucker learned that lesson the very hard way. "We bought a bunch of tanks from out of state," he says. "They weren't grandfathered in, but we set them anyway out of ignorance. We got fined. My big mistake was thinking that a tank was just a tank. It would have taken me five minutes on the phone to find out otherwise."

Whether you're running a start-up or planning to expand a decades-old gas business, cash—or rather the lack thereof—causes more problems than anything else, according to Milton. "Working capital was the biggest problem I faced. Managing for a major company, I never had to worry about money. You just worried about setting tanks and growing your business. I just never realized how much cash it took to get going. The money goes out the door like you would not believe. If you think you have enough money in your 401K to finance a start-up, think again." Milton says he was fortunate in finding private investors to fund his start-up.

And if you're thinking about buying an existing dealership, don't make the very expensive mistake Hunsucker made. He hired the wrong attorney. He didn't, and, he explains, "It cost me $40,000. We shook hands the day of closing, then got a call two days later saying that we hadn't bought the license to sell gas in our county. It was a hard lesson. Our attorney just didn't know that loophole."

These are just a few of the many lessons to be learned from the experiences of other dealers and distributors. Fortunately, you don't really need to go to the same school of hard knocks that they did. Instead, just ask a few of them what they've learned from their mistakes. You'll hear about their troubles and triumphs, their goofs and their glories. Just make sure the person you're talking to knows the business. As Milton points out, "Friends and relatives and everybody else wants to tell you how to do it. But somebody that's in real estate doesn't sell propane. Somebody who sells cars doesn't sell propane."

If you're going to learn from some else's mistakes, make sure they're the right ones.

Chapter 53

Industry Insights: Automotive Service
"Do your homework before you buy."

"Lots of times, being compassionate for people gets me in trouble," says Scott Hoffman, owner of Scott's Speed Shop in Hagerstown, MD. Scott's been selling parts and doing performance modifications on street rods, dragsters, and dirt track cars since 1974. He's seen his share of disasters created by somebody else and brought to him to straighten out. Being a customer-service kind of guy, he tries to solve their problem—which usually costs him money. "It's amazing the amount of things we get in here where we have to fix somebody else's mess-ups," he says. "We never come out on a job like that."

But what choice do you have? Turning customers away isn't exactly the best way to build a clientele. The solution is a combination of good customer communication—explaining what realistically can and cannot be done to solve their problem—and pricing the work so that you don't lose your shirt on the job. It's tough, especially when some customers' expectations aren't very realistic. "The greatest challenge is getting customers to understand what they can and can't do with some of the equipment," Hoffman observes. "Just because they see something for one vehicle, they think it's available for everyone. And people don't realize that some of the things they do in a half hour TV show can't really be done in thirty minutes."

Service with the sale

Parts installation and shop services may be the source of end-less headaches, but at least one parts retailer wishes he'd expanded into it several years ago. Harry Tillman, who has owned a speed shop in Aston, PA, for 27 years, says not offering installation has probably meant some lost opportunities. He's quick to add, though, "There are a lot of headaches with having a shop. With parts, if somebody brings it back with a complaint, you can just exchange it or give them a refund."

Craig Newport, who owns Cincy Speed Warehouse in Cincin-nati, OH, is considering expansion into shop operations, too. He's owned the retailer/wholesaler since 1993 and has about 8,000 square feet of retail and warehouse space. Newport is also trying to correct another mistake of omission he made a few years ago. "I wish we had computerized earlier," he says. "We tried it a couple of times in the past and we had problems with the system and I just said the heck with it. We went back to paper because that's what we know." Newport reports he is in the process of computerizing the operation now, with all the detail and extra work that entails. It was a step that had to be taken, however, because the paper-based operation was impacting revenue. "I'm sure it cost us a lot of sales. Someone would come in looking for something we should have in stock but didn't because we didn't have the computer reminding us to order it. He'd just go somewhere else."

Marketing through technology

Oddly enough, computers are quite often the source of regret in the automotive performance business. Don Wilkins, a partner in Wise Speed Shop, a St. Louis, MO, institution opened in 1961 reports, "I wish we had been involved in e-commerce sooner. We should have been more aggressive in our online strategy. We've been on the web for five years, but we're just now developing a site to sell online." He came to that conclusion after losing sales to Internet-based competitors. "There are a couple of major mail order parts companies in the country that do a tremendous amount of business online. They cut into our business in more ways than one. They not only attract customers with selection, but they also order in volumes that allows them to cut their pricing."

Tillman agrees that failing to devote at least some effort to building an online business was a mistake he made as well. He, too, is creating an e-commerce equipped website. In one month, he reports, it attracted nearly a quarter-million visitors.

The road to online retailing has a few potholes, too, though, as Steve Hoffman can attest. He's in the process of building a new web site, too—his second one. The mistake he made the first time around was contracting for a website, paying for it, then not getting what he ordered, specifically the ability to sell online. Besides hiring a firm that obviously wasn't paying attention, he says his mistake was "paying for the job before it got finished. Now I'm working with somebody new, and I told him I'm not paying for a thing until he gets it done."

Capital pitfalls

There are pitfalls in other kinds of capital expenditures, too, especially when it comes to shop machinery. Let's face it: at heart, most shop owners are gear-heads who think nearly all mechanical devices are cool. So when somebody comes up with a new frammis to recasterbrate a whoodiddis, you've just got to have one. And they're not cheap. "At one time, I said I'd never buy another tire machine, but now I have a new tire machine and a tire balancer that set me back $35,000," Hoffman says. He's still not sure how many times a year the machines will actually be used. Another problem with shop equipment, especially in this age of digitization, is that there are more things that can go wrong with the machinery. "Once a year, at least, you have to have the supplier come back and calibrate the machine. That's another added expense," Hoffman adds. "You didn't used to have to do that."

The way to protect yourself from that kind of mistake is to do your homework before you buy. "It's amazing how many equipment manufacturers are out there that sell sub-par stuff," Hoffman says. "I bought a programmable machine to evacuate and recharge air conditioning units for $6500 and it only worked three or four times. I had to go to the salesman's boss and tell him I wouldn't pay for it. He finally gave me one of half the capacity. It actually worked better."

Trust Your Instincts

Steve Dominguez, owner of Carolina Restyling and Upholstery in Charlotte, NC, says, "I wish I had read the hand-writing on the wall a little sooner," when asked to identify his biggest mistake.

He runs a 22,000-square-foot shop with thirteen employees that do both upholstery and body work. He regrets not taking the plunge into high-end custom retail work many years sooner than he did.

Dominguez had been in business for twelve years when I spoke to him, but spent the first several years concentrating on interior repairs and installations for auto dealers. "The dealer market changed dramatically in twelve years," he points out. "It's getting more and more difficult for dealers to do stock items. That's become the exception not the rule. They will do units when the customer requests and we're there for them on that." Most of his profit now, though, comes from retail customers.

"Our price points to the dealers have remained stagnant, even though our costs are going up," Dominguez says. "Vendors, fuel, and labor costs go up yearly but we're still at the same prices we were five or six years ago. Margins have been squeezed." But retail customers building their dream cars are usually empty nesters with the disposable income to get what they want and are willing to pay for quality work. "On the high-end custom work, you have much better margin," he says. "In hindsight, I wish we would have started the restoration side many more years ago."

That wouldn't necessarily have hurt his dealer business, he believes, since the dealers he serves now recognize that the Carolina Restyling technicians installing their sunroofs and leather seats are the same ones who do $200,000 custom jobs for retail customers. The quality of the work is still important to some dealers.

Another mistake, according to Dominguez, was subleasing his body shop operation for many years. "When you don't have control over the quality or the timeliness of the product, you run into issues," he says. "I saw those issues coming early on, but I was reluctant to jump in with both feet." When Dominguez finally took the plunge and took over the body work himself, he not only eliminated quality control problems but gained the ability to more fully serve his retail custom car customer.

Price with pride

Mobile GraFX owner Dan Baughn identifies a very common mistake that many craftspeople make: he sometimes hesitates to price his work for what he knows it's worth. The Central Valley, NY, shop owner started five years ago with a mobile van doing on-site truck lettering. Today he has a shop that does flaming and other auto body graphics as well as all sorts of stationary and rolling signage.

Like most restyling crafts, there are two ways to do graphics: quick and dirty or painstakingly perfect. Unfortunately, not all customers understand the difference, which makes it difficult for artists like Baughn to demand top dollar. The competition doesn't help, either. "It's tough when you've got guys working with no overhead so they can compete for a lot less," he says. "It doesn't come out as good as yours, but people don't understand that."

"Over time, I learned, although I probably still under-price myself on some jobs," he explains. "You learn what your value it."

Spend your time profitably

Shawn Krist owns Krist Kustoms in Fort Wayne, IN, where he has been specializing in custom interiors for the last seven years.

314

He made the mistake once of trying to be in two places at once, a feat not only impossible to accomplish but expensive to attempt.

"I hired a guy to work for me full time," he explains. "But it didn't work out nearly as well as I thought. The type of work we do is real detail oriented. If I hire somebody, I've got to watch half the time anyway. If I'm watching them, I might as well do it myself."

He hired the guy, Krist said, so he could spend more time attending to business matters. "But it got to the point where I was spending most of the day doing paperwork. I should have thought about the type of help I needed," he observes. "When he left, my wife took over most of the office work and I got back to the shop." Today he has a part-timer to help with overflow.

Get an education

Your mother said it, you high school counselor said it, and now Jeff Feinberg is saying it: Go to college! Feinberg owns East Coast T-Tops, where he installs and repairs sunroofs, T-tops, and Corvette roof panels. He's been in business thirty years and says right away that his biggest mistake was not going to college. He doesn't want you to go to school to learn Shakespeare, however; he believes it will make you a better business owner.

"The biggest mistake I made is having no marketing background," he says. "I concentrate on doing the work." If he'd invested the time in college businesses courses, Feinberg says, he would better understand how to grow and manage his revenues and profits. He'd have business skills as sharp as his technical skills and that would make his shop more successful.

Chapter 54
Industry Insights: Golf Course Operators
"It all begins with hiring the right people,
which is easier said than done."

Among the many variables golf course superintendents have to juggle very day, perhaps none is so complex as the people they manage. You probably face the same questions. Who do you hire? How do you get them to come to work every day? And persuade them to actually work while they're there? There questions are only the tip of the iceberg when it comes to employee matters, according to Chris Edmonson, Golf Course Superintendent at Pine Dunes in Frankston, TX. Edmonson summarizes the quandary: "To get the guys to work for you and produce, that's the biggest challenge for anybody. You can know everything there is to know about growing grass, but if you can't get your guys to do what you want, then it doesn't matter."

It all begins with hiring the right people, which is easier said than done. "Most of the people we hire don't have much education, so I basically sit down and talk with them for a while and try to get a feel for the kind of character they have," explains Phil Fitzgerald, Golf Course Superintendent of Steele Canyon, in Jamul, CA. New hires are on a ninety-day probationary period at Steele Canyon, as they are in many operations, but it seldom takes that long to tell if someone isn't going to perform, Fitzgerald says. "We've all hired people who didn't work out," he points out.

"Whenever it comes time for termination, be sure you have written documentation of the offenses and the reasons for being terminated," Edmonson warns. "I had to let a mechanic go, and he fought us on it through the Texas Workforce Commission, but luckily I had documentation stating the reasons for termination. If I hadn't had that, we would have had to pay the guy."

One of Fitzgerald's hiring mistakes was "a guy who faked a back injury. We finally ended up hiring a private eye to get some photos of him. We caught him moving furniture," he says. The pictures saved the company a lot of money in compensation claims.

"You never know if he or she is going to be a good worker until you get them out there and show them your ways," says Fred Travis, who oversees a staff of 150 as the Director of Golf Maintenance for nine courses at Barefoot Golf Resorts and The Legends Group in Myrtle Beach, SC. He says that a willingness to work is the most important quality to look for in a new hire: "One of the best employees I ever hired was a man who came up to me and couldn't speak of lick of English. He had a pair of blue jeans on that were about four inches too short on him and a pair of Sunday dress shoes. I could just tell by looking at him that he was hungry for work. I hired him and trained him to walk-mow greens, put cross-tie steps in, and he learned to do it all. He was probably one of the best physical laborers I ever hired."

Friends checking friends

Employees aren't the only humans with whom superintendents have relationships. There are also vendors. For just about
everybody, a friendly supplier is one you can trust. Of course, you
still check everything because, as Travis says, "I'm not saying
they're not honest, but they are going to make mistakes just like
everybody else. You have to check them."

Fitzgerald, who says he's used the same suppliers since he got
into the business twelve years ago, agrees that trust is important, as
is friendship. Still, he says, "I'm a big believer in spreading the
business around. That way you keep everybody in check. If you
stick with the same people all the time, you're not checking prices.
It's just a good idea to shop a little bit to make sure everybody's
staying in line. Even your friends."

It pays to do your homework when it comes to equipment,
too, whether you lease or buy it. Edmonson tells the story of a
huge turf slicer his predecessor bought, which he would like to use
but doesn't really have the crew to operate. "It basically sits there
taking up space in the shed," he says. Edmonson recently traveled
to the John Deere factory in North Carolina specifically to inspect
some machinery he was preparing to lease.

Fitzgerald is a big believer in looking before leaping, too. "I
research stuff real thoroughly before I buy. I usually have a shopping list when I'm going to the trade show so I can check everything out real well there. I talk to the reps and then we'll do some
demos before I buy anything. Normally, we'll get two or three

pieces of equipment in to compare so you get a chance to see it work."

Balance the budget

One of the most delicate balancing acts a superintendent is called on to perform is with his or her budget. On the one hand, you've got to please the customers. On the other, you've got to protect the owner's bottom line. The choices are tough. Nobody faces a more difficult market than Travis, who says, "If you don't have a good product, it hurts your business. We're in the resort business and we're in competition with a hundred and twenty golf courses at Myrtle Beach. You've got to beat them."

"I've been lucky to work for ownership that knows you have to spend money to have a quality product," Fitzgerald agrees. "But we've all had to tighten the screws the last few years with the economy and everything." So where do you tighten up? "I look at the things I can do without," he says. "For instance, changing out course accessories like pins and flags and cups three times a year instead of six. The last place I'll cut will be my fertilizer and chemical line."

"Don't cut what's going to hurt the turf," echoes Edmonson. "I hate to say it, but manpower's usually the first to go. I always try to keep the turf healthy and taken care of and if that means working long hours or hiring some part time guys, that's one thing. But don't ever short yourself on fertilizer or what you need to keep things maintained. You can't skimp on that."

In the end, it's the customer's experience on the course that's going to bring them back again with their wallet in their hand.

That's why professionals like Edmonson do more than just ride around the course with a notepad: "If you play the course once a week," he advises, "you'll see more than you'll ever see just riding around on a golf cart. I play to make sure I'm not missing something and to get the golfer's perspective. You don't have to play well, but you need to get out there and see what they're seeing."

Keep an open mind while you're looking around, Edmonson advises: "I see a lot of guys get into trouble by sticking to the same things all the time like clockwork and not being flexible. That's the biggest thing that gets people in trouble agronomically. In this business, you have to be flexible because conditions are changing all the time."

These are just a few of the many lessons to be learned from the experiences of other superintendents and you don't really need to go to the same school of hard knocks that they did. Instead, just ask a few what they've learned from their mistakes. You'll hear about their troubles and triumphs, their goofs and their glories. As Edmonson points out, "Superintendents are constantly helping each other out, whether it's talking about a problem that's happening or finding people. That's our biggest attribute."

Chapter 55
Industry Insights: Pizza Restaurants
"Even good recommendations aren't the total answer."

"When you talk about mistakes, the first thing that comes to mind are employees," according to Rob Raia, co-owner of six-year-old Borriello Brothers Thin Crust Pizza in Colorado Springs, CO. He says the mistakes begin during the hiring process, when the operator is so eager to fill a job that they overlook an applicant's weaknesses. "So you hire a guy and they can do one or two things good, but the things they do bad or can't do just overwhelm everything else," he says. That mistake is amplified when hiring on the recommendation of a friend or customer. Raia tells about hiring a customer's son and his friend, both seventeen. "The son lasted a little over two weeks," he relates. "The friend lasted a little longer. He made a career out of it. He lasted five weeks."

Cleve Williams, co-owner of an eleven-restaurant group built around the flagship Spanky's Pizza Galley & Saloon, in Savannah, GA, agrees. "Most hiring done from a recommendation by friends or family doesn't work out," he says. "If the recommendation comes from somebody in the business, it's better." Even good recommendations aren't the total answer. Williams says, "Any time you deal with entry level employees, you're going to have some difficulties." He learned to always put new hires on a probationary period.

Advertising trial and error

Marketing to keep your business growing is a mine field, too. Advertising mistakes are expensive and different operators have vastly different experiences with various media. "I started advertising this year," says Chicago's Pizza Metro owner Marco Schiavoni, who opened his thin-crust square-pan 20-seat pizzeria three years ago. He distributes flyers in surrounding neighborhoods, runs small ads in free-distribution newspapers, and pays for listings in nearby hotels. "The only thing that didn't work was Money Mailer. It costs too much money for a small place like me. I believe it works, but you have to be there all the time."

Williams' experience with direct mail was very different. "I've done very little advertising, but the Val-Pak coupons work much better than the newspaper."

Raia did some couponing, too, but it didn't work. He also runs a little radio but finds results very hard to track. When he tried an ad in the local college directory, though, he got great response. His most successful marketing experiment, though, was making direct calls on car dealers, who typically order in lunch for their staffs on Saturdays so they won't have to leave the lot on their busiest day. "I took free pizzas to a few car dealerships," he explains. "I talked to the manager about who ordered the food on Saturdays and made sure he got the free pizza. It cost me a few bucks, but the back side—to get an account off of it—is huge." He also drops off paper menus, because, as he says, "If you don't get them then, at least you made an impression. You're bound to get somebody off that dealership. Even if you don't get the big order, you're going to get somebody to try you for lunch or dinner."

Happy menu mistakes

Most operators fiddle with their menus as they constantly strive to please their customers' finicky tastes. Some new recipes crash and burn (a few literally), but mistakes can turn out to be fabulously successful, too. One of the happiest mistakes anyone ever made, according to Williams, was when Spanky's had some chicken breasts that were too large for their sandwich serving, so they trimmed off the tenders. Not wanting to waste the pieces, they fried them up in batter and chicken fingers were born, soon to be a nationwide craze. "The chicken fingers came from a mistake, and they became our number one seller," he says.

Schiavoni, who is opening a second location near Wrigley Field recently, tries to avoid menu mistakes by trying out new items on his customers before he makes a final decision. "Before I put something on the menu, I give it a try for a couple of months," he explains. "I give it away free to people and see the response. If they start to ask for it, I put it on the menu."

Raia has done some experimenting with the product, too. "We tried a different thing with our dough one time," he says. "We wrap individual balls of dough in plastic wrap, but once we tried not wrapping it at all, just leaving it covered in the dough tray. But there were too many variables that were affecting it. The temperature, for one. I thought it was going to be quicker, but it ended up costing us more time because the dough was all coming together and you had to cut it apart."

Going once...going twice

Equipment auctions offer great bargains, but the atmosphere isn't exactly conducive to well-considered decision-making. Sales are final, and so are the mistakes.

Rob Raia tells a sad tale: "I was at an auction and saw an old ice cream freezer—way old—but it worked so I bought it anyway. I brought it back and plugged it in and it died in a week. I hired a guy to fix it, and it ran for probably a month, then it became a shelf. We finally got it out of here a couple of months ago."

Marco Schiavoni had a similar experience: "Every time I go into my storage room, I see it right there. It's a beautiful refrigerated display case. I bought it during an auction but it's too big. It's been sitting in the basement for three years." He hopes to use it in his second location.

These operators didn't let their mistakes defeat them. Instead, they built on them the same way Jack Welch, the legendary ex-CEO of General Electric, built on his. Welch said, "I've learned that mistakes can often be as good a teacher as success."

About Dave Donelson

I've had four careers—each building on the one that came before it. The first was in small-market radio and television where I did everything from reporting the news and writing ad copy to selling spot schedules to local businesses. In the process, I learned a ton about how small companies work, how they interact with their customers, and what kinds of challenges they face—not just advertising and marketing problems, but personnel, finance, real estate, insurance, and even succession planning.

My second career was in national ad sales. I honed my selling skills competing for million-dollar budgets spent by the largest advertisers in the world. In addition to working with them and their advertising agencies on locally-executed campaigns in markets around the country, I built management skills as I climbed the ladder to eventually establish and run a nationwide sales organization with eleven offices and several hundred sales and support personnel.

Having built a company from the ground up for someone else, I decided it was time to strike out on my own, an urge that led me to found Sales Development Associates, Inc. (Donelson SDA), a management consulting firm that specialized in helping companies that were going through ownership changes and strategic transitions. My clients included one of every seven commercial television stations in the U.S. as well as companies in fields as diverse as heavy manufacturing and construction, magazine publishing, industrial sales, retail operations, and consumer services. I also took advantage of several opportunities to further test my entrepreneurial mettle by investing in a few select client companies and several successful start-ups.

Those investments allowed me to start my fourth career. For the last several years, I've been a writer and speaker, sharing what I learned with readers of some three dozen national newspapers and magazines and audiences at trade associations, professional group club meetings, and conventions of state and national organizations. In addition to the Dynamic Manager series, I'm the author of two novels. Learn more about me and the Dynamic Manager series at www.thedynamicmanager.com.

The *Dynamic Manager Handbooks* cover essential topics in convenient ebooks and include selections from all three *Dynamic Manager Guides*. Discover the entire collection of *Dynamic Manager Handbooks* by Dave Donelson at your favorite bookseller.

Management Skills

Profit Makers
The Dynamic Manager's Handbook On How To Run A Better Business
ebook ISBN: 978-1466136335

Finance Your Company
The Dynamic Manager's Handbook On How To Manage Your Cash For Growth
ebook ISBN: 978-1465757111

Strategic Hiring
The Dynamic Manager's Handbook On How To Hire The Best Employees
ebook ISBN: 978-1458100115

Employee Motivation
The Dynamic Manager's Handbook On How To Manage And Motivate
ebook ISBN: 978-1466019072

Family Business
The Dynamic Manager's Handbook On How To Build A Successful Family Company
ebook ISBN: 978-1466001190

Wit And Wisdom
The Dynamic Manager's Handbook Of Management Mistakes And Lesson Learned
ebook ISBN: 978-1465940797

Marketing and Advertising Skills

Five Rules Of Advertising
The Dynamic Manager's Handbook Of Small Business Advertising
ebook ISBN: 978-1458188007

Making Sales Appointments
The Dynamic Manager's Handbook On How To Reach Prospects
ebook ISBN: 978-1458116109

Overcoming Objections
The Dynamic Manager's Handbook On How To Handle Sales Objections
ebook ISBN: 978-1458172099

Closing The Sale
The Dynamic Manager's Handbook On How To Make Sales Happen
ebook ISBN: 978-1458159212

Sales TimeManagement
The Dynamic Manager's Handbook On How To Increase Sales Productivity
ebook ISBN: 978-1458014788

The Dynamic Manager's Guide To Marketing & Advertising:
How To Grow Sales And Boost Your Profits

This complete guide includes all the Dynamic Manager ebooks designed to help you grow your business with good marketing, advertising, and sales promotions. Hundreds of entrepreneurs and small business managers just like you tell how they learned to identify their best prospects, define their needs, and design marketing and ad campaigns that make the cash register ring.

- Market more effectively online—and off
- Beat the Big Box competition
- Find out what makes your customers tick
- Compete without chopping prices
- Tune up your publicity machine
- See seven ways to WOW your customers

Print ISBN: 978-1453889602
ebook ISBN: 978-1452491011

The Dynamic Manager's Guide To Creative Selling:
How To Make More Sales And Build A Super Sales Career

Creative Selling works in good economies and bad, whether you're selling widgets or financial services, roaming a nationwide territory or confined to a retail store. Learn the basic principles and hone your advanced selling skills in this combination edition of the DM Guide To Sales Techniques and the DM Guide To More Sales.

- Turn suspects into prospects and make prospects into customers for life
- Create demand from new customers and uncover new needs for existing ones
- Get easy cold call appointments and make sales on the first call
- Find the path around objections and close more sales without pressure
- Manage your time to make more sales and enjoy your super sales career

Print ISBN: 978-1460929667
ebook ISBN:978-1458114990

The Dynamic Manager's Guide To Practical Management:
How To Manage Money, People, And Yourself To Increase Your Company's Profits

Successfully managing a business takes knowledge, skills, and guts. Practical Management is based on interviews with retailers, manufacturers, service providers, wholesalers, restaurateurs, and others. Their stories of success—and failure—contain lessons for managers in every industry.

- Learn financial planning, find cash for your business, and manage your money through good times and bad.
- Use a variety of management techniques to manage change and maximizing profits.
- Follow the entire process from hiring and orienting employees to training, motivating, promoting, and even terminations.

Insightful case studies, company profiles, and insider advice from hundreds of business owners will help you take your company to the next level of success.

Print ISBN: 978-1463782054
ebook ISBN: 978-1466135536

One of the few things I enjoy as much as writing is speaking before groups of all kinds.

--Dave Donelson

"Wow! What a great presentation you made at our Annual Convention last week! We've heard excellent remarks and compliments on your session and hope you enjoyed doing it at least half as much as our delegates enjoyed hearing you."
--Oscar Rodriguez, Deputy Director Texas Association of Broadcasters

"Your seminar was great. Everyone in attendance seemed to enjoy themselves and I continue to hear very positive comments about your presentation. You were successful at interjecting some fun into the day, as well as providing our members with some very useful and much needed information."
--Sue Toma, Executive Director, Iowa Broadcasters Association

"...a timely and compelling presentation. Our evaluations indicate that it ranked high above average. Some of the positive comments we received referred to your upbeat tone, humorous style, inspirational words, and thought-provoking presentation."
--Debbie Griffin, President DFW Society for Marketing Professional Services

For more information
Email dave@thedynamicmanager.com